ALKAN

Vol. One: The Enigma

To my wife

Opening of an unfinished string quartet. Autograph signed by Alkan.
(Courtesy of Bibliothèque Nationale, Paris)

Ronald Smith

ALKAN

Volume One: The Enigma

*For Audrey Evelyn Bone,
with best wishes

Ronald Smith
21 . v . 79*

KAHN & AVERILL, LONDON

First published in 1976 by Stanmore Press Ltd
under their associated imprint: Kahn & Averill

Revised reprint 1977

Copyright © 1976 Ronald Smith

ISBN 0 900707 39 9

Photoset by Red Lion Setters
Holborn, London
Printed in Great Britain by
Biddles Ltd Guildford Surrey

Acknowledgments

I would like to express my warmest appreciation to those many friends and colleagues without whose help this book could not have been written. Notably, I must thank Richard Shaw, whose investigation, under the auspices of Edinburgh University, of Alkan's life and background coincided with my own researches. Most generously he placed the fruits of his tireless and imaginative labours at my disposal.

Jean-Yves Bras and Robert Collet also supplied me with invaluable information.

I am equally indebted to the following members of Alkan's family: Madame Rachel Guerret, Madame Jacqueline Cuzelin, Madame Dora Ray and Mrs Elizabeth Pierce.

I must thank Miss Jane Harington of the Royal Academy of Music Library and Richard Christophers of the British Museum for their personal kindness and help.

The Bibliothèque Nationale, Paris, also gave me every assistance.

John and Marie-France Sugden of the King's School, Canterbury translated and summarised over two hundred pages of baffling French handwriting and Alan Ridout and Richard Gorer both read the typescript, offering many useful suggestions.

Richard Gorer helped with the proof-reading and I am also grateful to Gerda Stevenson for her excellent realisations, from old photographs of Delaborde and Marmontel.

Finally, words cannot convey my gratitude to my wife, whose uncanny conversion of her husband's illegible handwriting into impeccable typescript was but one of the many tasks she undertook with tact, patience, fortitude — even enthusiasm.

RONALD SMITH
Canterbury 1975

Contents

Introduction

No recent event in the world of piano music has been more remarkable than the discovery by an ever-widening public of the works of Alkan. How is it that this exciting, this powerful, this strangely haunting, often surprisingly modern sounding music could have escaped attention for over a century? Not only has much of it been available in excellent editions but quite spectacular claims have been made for its originality and importance by such musicians as Busoni, Sorabji and Petri, one praising its sombre lyricism, another its biting satire while Isidore Philipp speaks of 'marvellous sonorities and such difficulties that reach the utmost bounds of piano playing.' Enough, one might imagine, to quicken the most jaded appetite. Yet, until the appearance in the late 1960's of the first gramophone records of such large-scale masterpieces as the *Concerto* and *Symphony for Solo Piano* the musical public had no means of testing the validity of Busoni's claim that Alkan, alongside Chopin, Liszt, Schumann and Brahms was one of the five greatest composers for the piano since Beethoven.

Critical acclaim, led by Harold Schonberg in America and by Roger Fiske and Stanley Sadie in the United Kingdom was immediate and decisive.

'As much of his best music is almost unplayably difficult,' wrote Dr. Fiske in *The Gramophone*, 'it is easy enough to see why he has never received his due as the most original composer for the piano of his century'.

Stanley Sadie, in *The Times*, emphasising Alkan's extraordinary dark power described the opening section of the *Concerto* as 'tough, severe, dramatic music, utterly unlike anyone elses.'

The time was right. An awakening interest was transformed into a consuming passion with urgent demands for more information about this lonely nineteenth century genius and his remarkable music. The purpose of this book is to attempt to fill in the tantalising gaps ... to examine those forces, internal and external, that threatened to tear Alkan apart, and to discuss some of the works the general music lover and student are likely to encounter.

1   Prodigy

'Charles-Valentin Alkan has just died. It was necessary for him
to die in order to suspect his existence. "Alkan," more than one
reader will say, "who is Alkan?" And indeed this paradoxical
man is all but unknown to our generation. This incomplete, this
interrupted destiny, this living burial of an artist of his calibre
... are they caused by the very character of this artist, by his own
desire, by his faults or even possibly by the exaggeration of his
qualities? Or can it be that French soil is unsuited to the
development of certain rare artistic plants? I cannot decide. I
am only required to recall the name and work of an artist
infinitely greater than thousands of his more celebrated and
praised contemporaries.'

So far as Alkan's life is concerned these words might well have
been written today. They are, in fact, quoted from an obituary
that appeared on the back page of the Parisian magazine Le
Ménéstrel on April the first, 1888. Nor was its author, Balthazar
Claes, alone in his reaction to this most elusive and
misunderstood of all French musicians. The following puzzling
sentence, first published in 1877, opens a short account of the
composer's life when Alkan was still very much alive.

'S'il est une physionomie d'artiste originale et curieuse à
ètudier entre toutes, c'est bien certainement celle de Ch.-V.
Alkan, dont l'intérêt se double d'une sorte de mystère et
d'énigme à pénétrer.' (Marmontel: les Pianistes Célèbres)*

---

*If ever there were a strange, eccentric artistic personality to study
it must surely be that of Ch-V Alkan, in whom interest is quickened
by a screen of mystery and enigma which surrounds him.

Antoine Marmontel, head of the piano department in the Paris
Conservatoire from 1848 to 1887 may, as we shall discover, have
had his own rather special reason for wishing to emphasise the
eccentricity of Alkan's personality, but clearly the task
confronting the modern biographer is daunting. Published
information is scanty and tenuous. Vital family documents were
destroyed by fire during the Paris Commune in 1871. Memories
of incidents handed down by word of mouth seem often
ambiguous or contradictory. But above all there is the man
himself, secretive, suspicious and with an almost pathological
revulsion against intrusion into his private affairs. Little wonder
that speculation and fantasy have filled the vacuum in our
knowledge of his life until there is a very real danger of the
legend devouring the man. Only persistent research and the
elimination of countless false trails has at last revealed, like the
completion of a complex mosaic, a design no less remarkable
than the myth it was intended to supplant: a character and a
career so strange, so perverse that the most febrile mind could
scarcely have invented them.

First of all, confusion about the various names by which the
composer has been known must be resolved. The two Christian
names Henri and Victorin which crept accidentally into early
biographies have proved stubbornly resistant. They are best
forgotten. He was registered simply as Charles-Valentin
Morhange but quickly replaced the latter by his father's first
name Alkan — John in English and meaning 'The Lord has
been gracious'. Signing himself C.V. Alkan aîné, he asserted his
position as the eldest of five brothers, all of whom, adopting the
name of Alkan, were destined to become distinguished Paris
musicians.

The family name of Morhange identifies them as Ashkenazi
Jews. Their ancestors had migrated from Eastern Europe in the
Middle Ages to form a self-governing community in the little
Alsatian town of that name. Here they endured conditions of
acute privation, the harshest in the whole of France. The more
enterprising left their poverty-stricken surroundings to seek
their fortune elsewhere. Many gravitated to Paris settling in the
ancient area known as the *Marais* which is still the centre of
Jewish life and culture in the capital. A few steps from the noisy
thoroughfare of the Rue St. Antoine and we are plunged into a

lost world of exotic bazaars, sombre bookshops and twilit cafés. This network of narrow streets in which Jewish craftsmen, shoemakers, carpenters, jewellers go about their daily work is delightfully scruffy; its atmosphere secret, timeless and self-contained; vibrant with the gentle activity of going about its business; aware, but quietly aloof. To this day the name Morhange is familiar in the *Marais* and Alkan's paternal grandfather, Marix Morhange, was probably well established there by 1780, the year in which the composer's father, Alkan Morhange was born. Marix's solitary appearance as witness at a family ceremony establishes his date of birth as 1748-49 just fifteen years before the death of his future grandson's beloved Rameau, last of the great French harpsichord composers. Of Marix's background we know nothing, although the subsequent academic and musical career of his son and the remarkable gifts transmitted to his grandchildren and their progeny, is highly suggestive.

Again, nothing seems to be known of Alkan Morhange's education and early career, but he springs suddenly and vividly to life at the age of fifty-two. Writing nearly half a century later Marmontel recalls his close association with the Morhange household; an association as yet unclouded by future events. Alkan's father, he tells us, ran a little boarding-school in the Rue des Blancs-Manteaux in the *Marais*, where young, mainly Jewish children received an elementary education in music and French grammar. He goes on to describe an environment which must have been ideal for the nurturing of a young, phenomenal talent. 'I can still see that little house of Monsieur Alkan Père, that patriarchal milieu in which flourished the talent of Valentin Alkan and where flowered his industrious youth. I was myself a boarder there for several months during a period when a group of young people, including Ravina and Honoré, were coming regularly for lessons in solfège and musical theory. It was a kind of juvenile annexe to the Conservatoire. What happy, carefree evenings spent in Valentin Alkan's company, that is, of course, before he had become the lonely recluse of his maturity. Gay, joyous and full of confidence, he shared all the enthusiasms and happy illusions of youth'.

Marmontel describes Alkan's father as hardworking and

intelligent but, alas, makes no mention of his mother. Her name was Julie Abraham and she was born in 1784 or 5 at Mousigny in the Moselle. Her marriage to Alkan Morhange had taken place on 12th April 1810, when he was about thirty, her senior by five years. Their first-born, Céleste (25.2.1812) was succeeded by five musical brothers of whom the first and greatest was Charles -Valentin born on the 30th November 1813.

Quite clearly a prodigious talent began to emerge at a remarkably early age and one can imagine the young Alkan practising elaborate vocal exercises (doubtless egged on by his big sister who was also in training for the sight-singing 'Olympics') almost before he could walk or talk. Not only was he accepted as a student at the Paris Conservatoire at the age of six, but a mere year and a half later was awarded his Premier Prix for solfège, a form of vocal musicianship considered indispensible in the Conservatoire. The professors themselves, headed by their principal, Cherubini, composed the exercises which often required a highly developed contrapuntal skill and were specially devised for a course of study extending over several years. The Morhange household, it seems, must have devoured and breathed solfège. Sister Céleste and brothers Ernest, Maxime and Napoléon all gained first prizes in this exacting art at the precocious ages of thirteen, fifteen, eleven and eleven. Napoléon in fact, eventually became *doyen* of solfège in which capacity he played an active part, until his retirement from the Conservatoire in 1896, in the training of such famous musicians as Bizet and Sarasate. The other brothers, including the youngest, Gustave Alphonse, each pursued careers as pianists, composers and teachers: that is except Ernest, whose flute playing, noted for its 'neatness of execution', won him first prize in this instrument at sixteen. He went on to play in the orchestra of the Théatre du Gymnase.

In 1821, the year of his solfège triumph, the young seven-and-a-half-year-old Valentin made his first recorded public appearance, singularly enough as a violinist. His choice of an 'Air Varié' by Rode, probably 'La Ricordanza', suggests considerable development, for the piece, like most of its genre, requires an elegant treatment of such skills as *spiccato* and syncopated bowings across the strings as well as a firm security in treacherous double stopping. Presumably he had also been

practising the piano in his spare time, for he was now accepted
as a member of Zimmerman's class where he began to lay the
foundation of that mastery which was later to become
unsurpassed.

Joseph Zimmerman (1785-1853) was, from 1826 to 1848, the
most celebrated piano teacher in the Conservatoire; but he was
much more. As a former pupil of the great Cherubini, esteemed
by Beethoven as the finest living stage composer, Zimmerman
was a man of the widest culture, an opera composer and a highly
respected contrapuntist. When one remembers that his later
pupils included César Franck, Ambroise Thomas, Gounod and,
in his last ten years, the youthful Bizet, the fact that Alkan
remained his favourite can hardly be ignored. A beautiful
pastel portrait of the young Alkan, now in the possession of his
brother Napoléon's descendants, was commissioned by
Zimmerman in honour of his brilliant pupil.

Was Alkan overworked as a child? According to the
Conservatoire register he was often away sick, and although
there is no reason to suspect more than the usual childish
ailments, he does seem later to have become highly neurotic
about his health. For the moment, however, nothing seemed to
impede his progress, and by 1824 he had scored his second
triumph with the even more coveted first prize for piano. It was
now becoming obvious that the ten-year-old boy was something
quite out of the ordinary, and Zimmerman lost no time in
bringing him to the attention of leading musicians like Rossini
who described him as 'that wonderful child'. While
Zimmerman was arousing the interest of influential benefactors
it was Alkan's father whose tactful initiative provided his son
with his early and necessary public experience. On the 2nd
April 1826 a concert 'Au benéfice du jeune Alkan âgé de onze
ans' (he was, in fact 12!) was organised at the showrooms of
Monsieur Pape. Thus started a close liaison between Alkan and
the piano-manufacturing industry which was to endure for the
rest of his long life. Apart from taking responsibility for such
administrative chores as advance publicity, printing, and the
engagement of supporting artists Alkan's father, probably
encouraged by Zimmerman, was at pains to seek the official
backing of the establishment. The young artist must have felt
highly gratified when he received the following letter and

212.
Mr. Alkan

CONCERT

AU BÉNÉFICE DU JEUNE ALKAN,

AGÉ DE 11 ANS,

Elève de M. Zimmerman,

Dans lequel il exécutera un Air varié de sa Composition.

On y entendra : Mmes. Pasta, Schutz, et Mlle. Alkan ;
MM. Rubini, Galli, Camus, Benazet, le jeune
Massard, et d'autres Instrumentistes des plus dis-
tingués de la Capitale.

J'ai l'honneur de vous prévenir que ce Concert aura lieu
le Dimanche 2 Avril prochain, à une heure, chez M. Pape,
Facteur de Pianos, rue de Valois, n°. 10, et rue des Bons-
Enfans, n°. 19.

Votre très-humble et très-obéissant Serviteur,

Rue Simon-le-Franc, N°. 10.

Paris, le   Mars 1826.

Announcement of Alkan's first concert.

testimonial from the Director of Fine Arts, Vicomte de la Rochefoucauld, a few days before the event: 'It is with real pleasure, sir, that I am taking the opportunity of giving you evidence of the quite special interest your talent arouses in me. In accordance with the wish you have expressed, I am subscribing to your concert the sum of 100 francs'. The testimonial reads as follows: 'The young Alkan, whose precocious talent is the subject of admiration for lovers of firm and brilliant technique on the piano, proposes to give a concert on April 2nd and is desirous of obtaining for his musical gathering a subscription from the Department of Fine Arts. This artist, aged only 11 years [*sic*], is granted the encouragement he requests. It is proposed, therefore, to subscribe to his concert the sum of 100 francs'.

Alkan appeared for the first time in the combined role of pianist and composer and one of his supporting artists was his sister Céleste.

Apart from his studies with Zimmerman, Alkan was also established in Dourlen's harmony class and achieved his 'hat trick' with a 'first' in harmony in 1827. He was now a 'veteran' of 13, assisting Zimmerman as repetiteur and being introduced by his proud teacher to the Paris salons. The most important of these 'soirées' were those given by La Princesse de la Moscova. In later years Alkan spoke with tenderness of the reception he received from this influential lady; but he also recalled a dark cloud which descended on one of these brilliant occasions causing him deep, if temporary distress. He noticed the presence of a handsome stranger some two years his senior. Later, this striking youth was also invited to the piano. Imagine Alkan's feelings when, on the very scene of his own personal triumphs, he was now made to witness a display of virtuosity such as he had never even imagined and one which relegated him to second place! Tears of vexation, followed by a sleepless night, were merely the outward manifestations of this first encounter with Liszt. It may well have been his most enduring lesson for, late in life, the ever-generous Liszt declared that Alkan had the greatest technique he had ever known, a view not so surprising to those familiar with such compositions as *Quasi Faust* and the fearsome *Trois Grandes Etudes* op. 76.

2 Virtuoso

Alkan was now 15 and faced with that lonely, often painful struggle to survive the cosseted and transitory glory of the wonder-child. The next five years were devoted to consolidating a reputation that was already enabling him to play with such famous artists as the 'cellist Franchomme with whom he and a leading Paris violinist, Alard, were soon to form a trio. It may well have been Franchomme, five years his senior and the future dedicatee of Chopin's 'Cello Sonata', who first introduced Alkan to the Polish master. Although Alkan's first publications date from the early '30's they were probably written still earlier. Consisting of showy fantasies like *Il était un p'tit homme* op. 3, they display little beyond the all-too-familiar drawing-room elegance of the period. According to Fétis the first real landmark was an orchestral concert in the Conservatoire in 1831 at which the seventeen-year-old soloist scored a big success with a piano concerto of his own composition. Could this, one wonders, have been the First Concerto da Camera, op. 10, and published in 1834? This is the first work of Alkan to show a distinctive creative personality and a grasp of form quite absent from those earlier compositions.

By 1833 a recently founded periodical *Le Pianiste* was closely following his activities: 'Alkan's musical and intellectual faculties have shown a remarkable development for some time' we are told, and shortly afterwards the same paper reviewed another performance of a concerto of his own composition: 'Remarkable for its form and style which are new'. The scherzo, the writer tells us, was encored and there follows an interesting description which tallies with no surviving concerto by Alkan:

'A simple, gracious muted song for strings is accompanied by a series of chords which, passing from octave to octave, sustains the melody and produces an effect as original as it is ravishing'. This is quite sufficient to identify the piano part as the second of Alkan's *Trois Andantes Romantiques* op. 13 which was also published independantly as *Caprice ou Étude* in C sharp'. Sure enough, we find included in one of Alkan's last programmes a study in C sharp for piano and orchestra. Unfortunately there is now no way of identifying the remainder of the concerto played in 1833. The strange habit of interpolating an attractive solo piece with added orchestral background within the framework of a concerto was once the common practice of such artists as John Field, but the whole incident also underlines the difficulty of establishing the identity of some of Alkan's early compositions.

Later this same year, on St. Cecilia's day, Alkan was entrusted with the important piano part in a performance of Beethoven's Triple Concerto with distinguished members of the Paris Conservatoire Orchestra. The conductor, Habeneck, target for some of Berlioz's most sarcastic quips was, nevertheless, one of the most famous and influential conductors of his day, having introduced the Beethoven symphonies in France. The review was not without reservations: 'We must compliment Alkan on having rendered in all its purity, if a little coldly, the composer's text'. In a later chapter we will examine in some detail Alkan's stature as a pianist. For the moment the following notice in the *Revue et Gazette Musicale* of his performance at a similar concert just two years later gives a good idea of those qualities most admired in his playing at the age of twenty-one: 'The piano sings deliciously beneath his fingers and it would be difficult to find more vigour, more clarity or more brilliance than in his distinct, pure playing in which myriads of notes fall like an enchanted shower of pearls and diamonds'.

So far Alkan's career as a virtuoso had been confined to Paris but at nineteen he now felt sufficiently encouraged to embark upon a strangely unlikely adventure ... at least, in the light of his later habits, it would seem utterly out of character. In 1833 he set out for London where he established contact with the publishing house of Cocks and Son which was later to bring out

several of his early compositions. Oddly enough there is no
evidence of his having played in London, no concert
announcement, no review: we do not even know where he
stayed, what he did or whom he met — that is with just one
exception. Early in 1834, and shortly after his visit, Henry Field
of Bath, a celebrated English pianist (not to be confused with
John Field, the creator of the Nocturne) gave a first
performance of Alkan's second Concerto da Camera in Bath
itself. The work, which is dedicated to Field, was also brought
out by Cocks that year. So presumably, Alkan met, and
probably played with Henry Field but, as far as we know, he
neither spoke of his English excursion nor of his return there in
1835. Even less is known about this second visit: just the chance
mention in a French periodical of a concert at which he played
with Moscheles and Cramer, two pianists worshipped by
London audiences. Alkan never left France again and soon
became reluctant even to leave the capital. It is significant to
read in *La France Musicale* of May 19, 1844: 'One by one the
great pianists leave the capital ... Chopin, Liszt, Thalberg ... we
do not yet know if Alkan will remain faithful to his beloved
Paris'.

Between his two visits to London Alkan consolidated his
reputation still further with a final first prize, this time for
organ.

* * * * * *

Alkan now decided the time was right to forsake his parents'
home in the *Marais* for that most fashionable centre of artistic
life in the capital, the Square d'Orléans. Such was the prestige
of its inhabitants, from writers like Alexandre Dumas and
Joseph d'Ortigue to the ballerina Marie Taglioni, that the
colony had been described as 'Une petite Athènes'. Here Alkan
would live on equal terms with the celebrated pianists
Kalkbrenner and Zimmerman, and later, when George Sand
and Chopin moved into the square, he was to become Chopin's
next door neighbour. Alkan and Chopin had become lifelong
friends since the early 1830's. They were similarly fastidious,
shared the same artistic ideals and enjoyed the same
entertainments. Chopin gives details of one such outing with his

friend: 'I went with Alkan to see Arnal at the Vaudeville in a new play by M. Duvert called 'Ce que femme veut'. Arnal, amusing as ever, tells his audience how he wanted to have a p — when he was in the train but could not get out before reaching Orléans. He doesn't utter a single improper word but everyone understands and it's a scream. He says the train stopped once and he wanted to get out, but he was told they were only "stopping to take in water for the engine" and "that was not at all what he wanted" — and so on.

According to Marmontel, Chopin, who was not prodigious with his affection, counted Alkan high on the small list of his confidants. In 1848 when Chopin was in Britain escaping the Paris revolution he wrote anxious letters about his friend's safety and even remembered him on his death-bed bequeathing to Alkan and another musician his uncompleted piano method. Alkan was, for his part, fascinated by the Polish genius, especially by the fierce national element in his compositions. His opinion of Chopin's playing, which he considered inimitable, will be discussed in a later chapter; and he and Chopin also enjoyed playing together. On one occasion Zimmerman, Chopin and his pupil Gutmann (the giant-fisted dedicatee of his master's 3rd Scherzo) all collaborated with Alkan in a performance of the latter's eight-handed arrangement of Beethoven's Seventh Symphony. Chopin survived this alarming event on 3rd March 1838 but a few years later pleaded insufficient strength to take his part in a repeat performance.

By the time of Alkan's arrival in the Square d'Orléans, he and Liszt were also on friendly terms, earlier rivalry having been forgotten. An article about Liszt published in 1835 mentions that his friends included Berlioz, Hiller, Mendelssohn, Alkan and Chopin; but although Alkan doubtless profited from Liszt's presence and collaboration at his concerts, he certainly shared a little of Chopin's envy at their friend's meteoric rise to fame, and some of his scepticism about his method of boosting it. Few of Liszt's colleagues could resist his spell-binding personality: few remained uninfluenced by his generosity. Yet such fastidious artists as Chopin and Alkan must often have felt their hackles rise at some of the antics with which the 'King of Pianists' would hypnotise his audience — that is, of course, before he became the 'Grand Seigneur' of later years. The following description quoted from Sacheverell Sitwell's book on the composer, gives an impression of Liszt's playing in Paris in 1835:-

'I saw Liszt's countenance assume that agony of expression, mingled with radiant smiles of joy, which I never saw in any other human face except in the paintings of our Saviour by some of the early masters: his hands rushed over the keys, the floor on which I sat shook like a wire and the whole audience was wrapped in sound, when the hand and frame of the artist gave way. He fainted in the arms of the friend who was turning over the pages for him and we bore him out in a strong fit of hysterics. The effect of this scene was really dreadful. The whole room sat breathless with fear, 'till Hiller came forward and announced that Liszt was already restored to consciousness and was comparatively well again. As I handed Madame Circourt to her carriage we both trembled like poplar leaves, and I tremble scarcely less as I write this'.

Liszt was, of course, a great champion of other peoples' music, yet there seems no evidence that he played a note of Alkan in public. As one of the very few pianists then capable of meeting the challenge of his friend's finest works he might well have turned the tide in Alkan's favour. For his part Alkan had a pretty poor opinion of Liszt as a composer. Even so, the two artists were not without mutual influence. Playing, such as Liszt's famous performance in 1836 of his arrangement of the *March to the Scaffold* (a *tour de force* which Hallé tells us surpassed even the splendour of Berlioz's original orchestration) probably taught Alkan more than ten years in the Conservatoire about the possibility of turning his piano into an orchestra. An examination of Alkan's Grande Sonate, on the other hand, soon reveals that the composer of the B minor Sonata must have been familiar with this little-known masterpiece written just six years earlier.

An important batch of compositions from Alkan's pen was published in 1832, including *Trois Études de Bravoure* op. 12, *Trois Andantes Romantiques* op. 13 and *Trois Grandes Études* (later re-named *Trois Morceaux dans le genre pathétique*) op. 15 which he dedicated to Liszt. This extraordinary but strangely uneven work consisting of three pieces entitled *Aime Moi*, *Le Vent* and *Morte* came in for some pretty harsh criticism from Schumann who described it as 'false, unnatural art … In *Aime moi* we have a watery French melody with a middle part unsuited to its title; in *Le Vent* there is a chromatic howl over an idea from Beethoven's 7th Symphony; and in the last we have a crabbed waste overgrown with brushwood and weeds, the best of it borrowed from Berlioz ...' Liszt, the dedicatee, could afford to be more generous. In an extended, complimentary but not uncritical article in the *Revue et Gazette*, 22nd October 1837, he finds the first piece 'simple, tender and full of melancholy': the second 'marvellously conveys the sound of those prolonged winds which moan monotonously for whole days.' Liszt analyses *Morte* at some length but concludes that, although it contains some beautiful things, Alkan seems encumbered by detail. Both he and Schumann remark on the fact that the whole work is published without tempo indications and dynamics. To twentieth century ears *Morte*, with its oppressive use of the *Dies Irae* and its sombre bell effects, which so strangely foresadow *Le Gibet* by Ravel, is by far the most telling of these pieces and the one most indicative of Alkan's later development.

On the 3rd March 1838, at that same concert at which Beethoven's 7th was performed, Alkan defied Schumann's accusation of plagiarising the Symphony's Allegretto by playing *Le Vent*. The performance was highly praised by the veteran critic Henri Blanchard as 'a delicious conception of descriptive music' adding, perhaps a little untactfully that Auber, in his ingenious portrayal of snow does not approach so near the truth. Auber was later to become head of the Conservatoire and this comparison could not have endeared Alkan to him. *Le Vent* may not be one of Alkan's best pieces but it caught the imagination of several later pianists like Adela Verne and Harold Bauer whose performance of it, around the turn of the century, was said to be 'electrifying'.

By the end of 1838 Alkan's *Trois Scherzi* op. 16, his *Six Morceaux Characteristiques* and the monstrous *Trois Grandes Etudes*, for the hands separately and reunited — later to be given the misleading opus number of 76 — were all in print. The impressive study for right hand alone must remain one of the most appallingly difficult pieces ever written and although Busoni played the study for left hand, and Rudolf Ganz the powerful moto perpetuo which reunites the hands, no public performance of the right hand study has yet been traced. The Three Scherzi, with their persistant rhythms and bold clean-cut outlines, are among the most attractive of Alkan's early works and are well worth playing, even if only for the irresistible trio of the first scherzo. Again and again one finds oneself returning to this delicate invocation of chiming bells, their falling cadences melting elusively into a shimmering haze of pedal-held sound.

The Six Characteristic Pieces, later incorporated into *Les Mois* op. 74, are early examples of Alkan's genius as a miniaturist and lie well within the scope of the amateur pianist. This is the only other work of Alkan that Schumann reviewed. One of these pieces entitled *L'Opéra* cleverly parodies French Grand Opera of the day and it struck a sympathetic chord in Schumann who had been busily castigating its most likely target, Meyerbeer, during those last two years. Schumann was far less enthusiastic about the other pieces which failed to satisfy his quest for emotional warmth and he adds a sting to the tail of his review, which concludes: 'The composer may be an interesting player who well understands the rarer effects of his instrument, but as a composer only the severest studies will enable him to make much progress, for he sinks too frequently into mere superficiality'. This harsh criticism may be justified in the light of Schumann's own standard of taste: but here a comparison with his review of Berlioz's *Fantastic Symphony* is instructive. Those very elements he found disturbing in Berlioz like 'flat and common harmonies, unclean and vague ones ... and some that sound bad, tormented and twisted' would have seemed to him the very stuff that Alkan's music was made of. The cold, stark realism that we now so admire in Alkan must have struck Schumann simply as tasteless incompetence.

We have no way of knowing if Alkan saw these reviews, which had appeared in the *Neue Zeitschrift für Musik* in May 1838 and May 1839, but he certainly never bore Schumann a grudge on their account. Perhaps, as we shall see in the next chapter, he was far too engrossed in personal matters to worry about bad notices.

3 Delaborde

Delaborde is a name not unknown to connoisseurs of Alkan's music, for it appears on the outer cover of the familiar Costallat-Billaudot edition of the composer's works. Otherwise very little is known about him, which is a pity.

Elie Miriam Delaborde was born in Paris on 8th February 1839 and was destined to become one of France's leading pianists. He studied with Alkan, Moscheles and Henselt, but in certain French musical circles it has been loudly whispered that his link with Alkan was rather more intimate than that of pupil and teacher. The claim that Delaborde was Alkan's natural son has been passed on and accepted by pupils of Isidore Philipp, the other name which appears on the title page of Alkan's music. No one seems ever to have questioned this relationship, yet it has proved stubbornly difficult to confirm. To start with no official document could be traced to prove Delaborde's identity; neither birth, marriage nor death certificate was issued in that name and investigation under the names of Alkan and Morhange has proved equally unproductive. Indeed, from a legal point of view Delaborde seems never to have existed, but such a disadvantage in no way inhibited him from pursuing a distinguished musical and artistic career or from living a highly colourful life as sportsman, amorist and naturalist. He was a champion swimmer, a passion he shared with his neighbour, Bizet. Indeed the death of Bizet seems to have been accelerated by a swimming expedition with Delaborde in the Seine. Furthermore the suspicion that Delaborde was at that very time having an affair with Madame Bizet finds ample confirmation in the recent discovery by Jean-Yves Bras of a marriage

announcement which appeared in a French magazine not long
after the composer's death, between Delaborde and Bizet's
widow.

   This event, however, did not take place, and when Delaborde
did eventually marry, on the 20th March 1901, at the age of 62,
it was to a lady with the resounding name of Marie Thérèse de
Courchant des Sablons. One can only hope she shared some of
her husband's unusual enthusiasms for it must have been a
unique and somewhat unnerving household. Delaborde's steady
stream of pupils seemed undeterred, however, by the presence
of two mighty apes who roamed his studio; and when the war of
1870 drove him to giving concerts in London he was
accompanied by his retinue of 121 parrots and cockatoos. Can
one reasonably believe that so extrovert and sturdy a character
could conceivably be the son of the ever-ailing, introverted
Alkan?

   Philipp clearly had no doubts about the relationship and it
was from Philipp too, that the veiled suggestion that
Delaborde's mother was a lady of high birth gave us our first
clue to her shadowy identity. From the same source it was also
intimated that Delaborde bore Alkan a bitter grudge for
denying him full legal status and that he was only reluctantly
persuaded to add his own, illustrious, name to Philipp's on the
cover of his 'father's' music.* This being so, it is difficult to
understand why Delaborde troubled to introduce Alkan's latest
pédalier works to London audiences in 1871, gave duet
performances with him in Paris or accepted the dedication of
his *Bombardo-Carillon*, that monstrous pedal-board duet for
four feet alone which caused Rudolf Ganz such embarrassment
when he tried it out with a lady pupil. Raymond Lewenthal,
who studied with a pupil of Delaborde, accepts the filial
relationship without question, adding that father and son
shared Alkan's apartment; but he gives no clue as to his source
of information. We do know, however, that Delaborde was one
of the very few people who had free access to the composer in
his later years.

---

*A former pupil of Delaborde, Gabrielle Fleury, told Robert Collet,
that her teacher was, indeed, the natural son of Alkan. This was later
confirmed by Philipp who added: 'Il détestait son père.'

This is how Alexandre de Bertha, a Hungarian pianist describes his first meeting with Alkan: 'It was at the beginning of 1872 that M. Delaborde, the superb pianist and eminent professor at the Conservatoire introduced me to Alkan with an eagerness all too rare among colleagues'. Nowhere in Bertha's long account of the composer is there the slightest hint of a father and son relationship. Delaborde was, of course, still very much alive in 1909 when this article was published, so either Bertha was unaware of his friend's identity or was preserving a well-guarded secret. Furthermore, there is only one most casual reference to Delaborde in a vast collection of recently discovered letters written by Alkan and spanning the crucial thirty years from Delaborde's early teens:- letters in which Alkan often compares his own personal isolation to others' family responsibilities. He did, however, remember Delaborde in his will, identifying him as Elie Miriam dit Delaborde and it may have been this information that set Jean-Yves Bras on the fruitful track of Delaborde's elusive mother. Monsier Bras, whose major investigation of Alkan's life and background is eagerly awaited, has most generously provided the following information: 'Elie Miriam dit Delaborde was born on the 8th February 1839, the son of Lina Eraîm Miriam rentière (a lady of means) living in Paris: father unknown.' The name of Delaborde, M. Bras suggests, may have been adopted from his foster mother who was living in Brittany during his childhood and to whom the boy was very attached. He also confirms that the only known official intimation that he was related to Alkan is his citation in Alkan's will. In the face of such scanty legal information one is obliged to fall back on circumstantial evidence and this is strong. Apart from his musical ability Delaborde was a fine painter, a gift that has persisted up to the present day in the Alkan-Morhange family. Alkan's elaborate *Marcia Funebre sulla Morte d'un Pappagallo* written, incidentally, when Delaborde was about nineteen, suggests that he was also a parrot fancier. Again a penchant for birds and animals persists in the Alkan family. But surely the most conclusive evidence that Delaborde was, indeed, Alkan's son is that no one has ever denied it, no other father has ever been suggested and the family itself has never questioned the relationship, including Elie Miriam dit Delaborde in the family tree.

Elie Miriam Delaborde
(Artist's realisation from a photograph:
courtesy of Bibliothèque Nationale, *Paris)*

* * * * * *

During the 1830's Paris had become the centre of a unique
explosion of pianistic talent. Stars like Chopin, Liszt, Thalberg
and Kalkbrenner could all be heard and compared within the
space of a few days, not only separately but often sharing the
same platform in a kind of pianistic jamboree. The following
event is typical: 'On April 30th (1837) the young César-Auguste
(Franck) aged fourteen, is to be found appearing on the concert
platform on an equal commercial basis with three of the best
known virtuosi of the time, the pianist Pixis, now nearing fifty,

the celebrated Alkan and the illustrious Franz Liszt ...'

The 'celebrated Alkan' was himself only twenty-four but fast becoming recognised as the leading French pianist. His future position in the Conservatoire, where his salary had now been increased to 1,000 francs, seemed hardly less assured. It was here, a year later, that he again met César Franck, but in rather different circumstances. Alongside the ageing Cherubini he was one of the examiners obliged to disqualify his young colleague for overstepping the regulations in the piano competition. Franck, eager to show off his transposing powers, had given a perfect rendering of the difficult sight-reading test, but in a remote key. Accordingly he 'failed' to qualify for the coveted first prize, but in recognition of his feat was given a 'Grand prix d'Honneur' as a specially created award. Perhaps Alkan had a hand in placating the rigid, regulation-conscious Cherubini on the boy's behalf, for Franck was not so generously treated three years later when he pushed his luck still further in the organ prize by combining two unofficially related subjects in an improvised fugue.

By the end of the decade Alkan's brilliance as a pianist was being matched by his ambition as a composer and the publication of his latest piano works in 1837 and 1838 marked a bold advance. In his threefold capacity of composer, performer and teacher Alkan had reason to feel reassured. His concert on 3rd March 1838, at which his distinguished guest artists included Chopin, must have been a memorable occasion: 'This brilliant evening' wrote the *Revue et Gazette* 'maintained for M. Alkan the twofold reputation he has already won as instrumentalist and composer. The large audience who flocked to hear him were unanimous in their enthusiasm'.

How little could this large, enthusiastic audience have realised their privilege: for they had just witnessed the end of Alkan's career as a virtuoso. Quite suddenly, without warning, his name vanishes from the pages of French musical periodicals and does not re-appear until he is over thirty. It is most puzzling. Was he suddenly smitten by some strange and protracted illness? If so no one has ever breathed a word of it and there is not the slightest hint that his health, at twenty-five was anything but robust. Could it be that he was becoming increasingly aware of his creative genius and simply felt the urge to devote more time to composition? Indeed, these mysterious and silent six years were highly productive; and not only so far as his music is concerned. Is it sheer coincidence that Alkan's self-imposed withdrawal from the Paris musical fray should date from the months immediately preceding the birth of Delaborde? Assuming he was Delaborde's father, and there now seems little reason for doubting the relationship, is it not feasible that he may have suffered a violent upheaval in his personal life: one which could have set up the preliminary tremors of that gradual change in his personality which would not only throw him off course but would ultimately plough his career into the ground? We can know nothing, of course, about the nature and depth of his relationship with the elusive Lina Miriam. Alkan always kept his private life very much to himself, and it is even possible that his closest associates and family knew little of a liaison which was to remain the composer's most jealously guarded secret.

Alkan never married.*

---

*Even as this book goes to print the author has just had the pleasure, while introducing Alkan's music in Australia, of meeting Mr. Cyril Ray, the great-grandson of Napoleon Alkan. Mr. Ray adds the following information about Delaborde's mother, which confirm our suspicions. Although her name was never divulged she was understood to have been a pupil of Alkan, a lady of high social standing . . . . and already married.

4 A Lost Symphony

On 14th April 1844, the following notice appeared in *La France Musicale*: 'We are happy to announce that Alkan has at last decided to give a concert on the 29th of April in the Salle Erard. Everyone knows of Alkan's superiority as a composer: now they will have an opportunity to judge for themselves his superiority as a performer'.*

Apart from being Alkan's first and only known solo recital the programme itself is of great interest. He opened with two movements from his *Second Concertino*, a solo adaptation, perhaps, of his *Second Concerto da Camera*, already published in England. But there is clearly some muddle, for although this recital was not reviewed in *La France Musicale*, we are told the following November, in its news section, that Alkan's 'magnificent Concerto, excerpts from which had produced such a huge sensation at his recital last winter, is soon to be published'. No concerto by Alkan *was* published during the 1840's and so the identity of this 'sensational' work must remain a mystery. It was followed by five equally unidentified *Petits Morceaux* which were played without break, and then came a Bach Gavotte, a Scarlatti Allegro and Alkan's own transcription of the minuet from Mozart's G minor Symphony. The Bach and Scarlatti may also have been arrangements but not, one assumes, the next two

---

*Although this announcement gives the impression that Alkan was a stranger to the Paris public, Hugh Macdonald's researches have yielded information about an earlier re-appearance on 27 Feb., 1844. d'Ortigue's review is of special interest as it mentions hitherto unknown and missing works, including quintets and sextets. According to Escudier, Alkan's April recital was rapturously received by a distinguished audience which included Chopin, Liszt, Sand and Dumas.

items: the Rondo from one of Beethoven's Sonatas op. 31, and
Weber's *Moto Perpetuo*. The recital ended with four important
first performances: *Air de Ballet, Nocturne, Saltarelle* and
Alleluia.

As these were all about to appear in print as his op. 22 to 25
one suspects that his publisher may have had a hand in
persuading Alkan to break his six year's silence. The *Saltarelle*
with its hair-raising leaps and furious energy quickly caught the
fancy of a sensation-loving public. Only a month after their
publication a certain Josephine Martin introduced all five of
Alkan's latest works to Paris including the *Gigue* op. 24, which
the composer seems to have omitted from his programme.
Playing on a magnificent new seven-octave Pleyel concert grand
she produced 'a powerful and elegant sonority' and was given a
standing ovation. The *Saltarelle* in particular was 'interrompu à
chaque reprise par les applaudissments frénétiques'. This
ecstatic notice in *La France Musicale* ends by saying; 'There will
soon be no pianist unacquainted with these latest brilliant
productions by Alkan'. Few artists can so thoroughly detach
themselves from public recognition as to remain indifferent to
such appreciation and Alkan was sufficiently encouraged to
plan further concerts during the next season and, more
important, to throw himself with renewed vigour into his
creative work.

On 27th October 1844 *La France Musicale* gives further news
of his activities and intentions: 'Alkan's latest compositions are
enjoying an enormous success and, encouraged by the
enthusiastic acclaim he received at his concert last season, this
great artist has consented to appear again this winter with new
masterpieces including a four-handed Fantasy based on *Don
Juan*, and two important études, *Le Preux* and *Le Chemin de
Fer*. Moreover he has just completed two Marches which he
introduced to a private audience of friends and we declare them
among his finest works yet for the piano. Above all, the
controlled verve and power with which he played the *Marche
Héroique* are characteristic of a talent which unites all the
factions in their admiration.' The two Marches did not appear
until December 1846 when they were published separately, with
a dedication to his pupil La Duchesse de Montebello as *Marche
Funèbre*, op. 26 and *Marche Triomphale*, op. 27 ... an opus

number already given to *Chemin de Fer* by a rival publisher. Alkan must have known Berlioz's great *Symphonie Funêbre et Triomphale* for massed bands, which received several performances in Paris during the early 1840's, yet, apart from their titles and an expression of public, rather than private emotion, Alkan's Two Marches have little in common with the Symphony. The facile description of Alkan as 'The Berlioz of the Piano' should not, in fact, mislead us. Both composers, it is true, discovered unheard-of sonorities for their very different media; both imbued a familiar language with new and disturbing power; yet even a common preoccupation with the darker shades of human experience only highlights the difference in their personalities. Humphrey Searle makes this admirably clear when he speaks of 'that element of "terribilità" which in Berlioz generally takes the form of wild devilment, in Alkan of icy restraint'. The Funeral March, with its spare textures, its hypnotically repeated rhythms and its telling use of a growling bass register in imitation of muffled drums, is a remarkable early example of Alkan's uniqueness in this respect.

So far the composer's growing reputation had been confined to solo piano pieces or works in which the piano played a dominant role. The sole exceptions were two unpublished cantatas dating from 1832 and 1834 and a *Pas Redoublé* for military band dated 1840. The former remain a sad monument to two youthful attempts at the Prix de Rome whereas the occasion that prompted the latter must remain a mystery. Far more important are two fine chamber works which he published in 1840 and 1841 but which seem to have passed unnoticed. Both the *Grand Duo* for violin and piano with its blood-thickening slow movement marked 'l'Enfer' (hell) and the impressive Trio, a favourite with Mendelssohn who enjoyed playing the piano part, are unique in their own special way. Although they made little immediate impact in Paris, due, no doubt, to Alkan's temporary absence from the concert scene, they show that by the early 1840's he was beginning to feel the urge to test his creative powers on a broader canvas.

Yet they hardly prepare us for an arresting announcement in *La France Musicale* on 7th November 1844. 'Alkan has now written a Symphony for full orchestra on which he is pinning his highest hopes. The season will not pass without a performance'

... but the season did pass without a performance ... and the
next season and the one after that ... and had it not been that
Alkan showed the manuscript to Léon Kreutzer, son of the
well-known dedicatee of Beethoven's Violin Sonata, the very
existence of Alkan's Symphony, as a completed work, must have
remained doubtful. This is how Kreutzer describes it in an
extended article about Alkan which appeared in the *Revue et
Gazette* in January 1846: 'The unpublished Symphony, which
M. Alkan was willing to show me, borrows nothing from the
capricious forms which the modern symphony has adopted.' He
then gives a detailed analysis of each of the Symphony's four
movements. The first, he tells us, is notable for its highly
organised development section, and he also singles out a striking
effect in the second subject which involves a pedal-point on the
woodwind. There follows a spirited Scherzo with a particularly
charming Trio. Kreutzer is most revealing when it comes to the
Adagio, although he could little have realised the significance
for Alkan of certain Hebrew characters in red ink which
decorated its first page. It was a verse from Genesis, Alkan
informed him, no less: 'God said let there be light and there was
light'. In a detailed comparison with the opening of Haydn's
Creation Kreutzer concludes that where Haydn scores with his
extraordinary inspired depiction of 'chaos' it is Alkan who is far
more convincing in his announcement of the 'explosion of light'.
He writes: 'The crescendo is superlatively achieved. The wind
unisons mingled with rapid scales produce the most grandiose
effect'. Kreutzer found the Finale less impressive in ideas but
highly skilful in treatment. The manuscript of Alkan's B minor
Symphony has long since disappeared and although hope of its
re-discovery one day has not been abandoned it is likely to
remain a tantalising mystery. Only the solo parts of the two
Concerti da Camera have survived although we do know that
the First was with small orchestra and the Second with strings
alone. The manuscript of the *Pas Redoublé* shows a skilled use
of heavy brass but it is far too limited, musically, to shed any
useful light on Alkan's orchestration. Some imaginative
woodwind writing, however, in the *Marcia sulla Morte d'un
Pappagallo* of 1859 suggests that his orchestral writing might
have been just as pungent and direct as his treatment of the
piano.

5 The "Grande Sonate"

At the beginning of 1838 Alkan's career as a virtuoso had reached its peak and collapsed. Now, as 1844 was drawing to its close there seemed every sign that he was to achieve his first real break-through as a composer. Stimulated, no doubt, by the success of his latest piano pieces he was caught up on a wave of creative energy which had just reached its climax with the B minor Symphony. But Alkan's destiny was not written in the stars: rather was it the child of his own complex nature, his ambivalence and his over-sensitive reaction to the vagaries of life.

On March 1st and 30th April 1845, he gave two important public concerts at the Salle Erard. Although appearing in every item, Alkan shared the programme with supporting artists including his brother Napoléon who, at eighteen, was also starting to make a considerable name as a concert pianist. A generous number of his own compositions were interspersed with classical works by Mozart, Beethoven, Schubert and Mendelssohn. We are told nothing of public reaction or support but the only performance to receive unstinted praise from the *Revue et Gazette* was the one with which he opened, the Adagio from Hummel's B minor Concerto performed with its original orchestration of four horns and low strings. After the euphoria of the previous year it must have struck Alkan like a cold shower to be told publicly that his playing 'lacked breadth, passion, poetry and imagination'; that his choice of music was 'old-fashioned' (a Schubert minuet) or 'drily scholastic' (a Mendelssohn fugue); but worse was to follow. His compositions were simply: 'the work of a man stirred by the cold; the systematic ... one who is occupied a great deal more by his own impressions than by those which he might produce on his audience.' Once more Alkan retired into his shell.

The following year saw the appearance of Kreutzer's long article about Alkan, the one in the *Revue et Gazette* in which the Symphony is analysed. Kreutzer also throws an interesting light on some of the adverse criticism of Alkan's latest concerts. 'Artists' he tells us 'appreciate his talent as a pianist better than the public. This was quite clear at the concerts he gave in the Erard "salons".' While applauding Alkan's conviction that he must lead, not follow public taste, both in his playing and in his choice of repertoire, Kreutzer feared that Alkan's zeal in this direction bordered on despotism and that his campaign against 'the false, the convulsive, the affected and the portentous' sometimes robbed him of inspirational freedom when playing in public. He also discusses Alkan's attitude to his career, its virtues, its dangers. He contrasts the worldly reputations of those who nurture their careers with the lot of the true artists whose lives are dedicated to contemplation and study. 'These latter' he writes 'having spent too much time on their work to spend any part of it on publicity and canvassing become a little disgusted with a public which does not come and seek them out. They continue, all the same, to perfect their own works but do nothing to promote them thus dedicating them to obscurity. Some time ago we told our readers of M. Reber who carries this need for obscurity almost to the lengths of a passion. Valentin Alkan is another of these misanthropes of the musical world'.

There is much common sense in Kreutzer's reasoning which is as relevant today as it was then: yet his sympathetic appraisal of Alkan's position and the gentle advice that he should re-think it is surely mistaken. A complete artist can only be true to himself. To ask him to be more 'realistic' is simply an invitation to do just that which he cannot do ... to compromise.

Although Alkan made no further bid to woo the Paris musical élite during the following three years he continued to attract the attention of the *Revue et Gazette*. On 25th July 1847 a further major article was devoted to him and this time the author was none other than its founder, the highly respected Fétis himself. His review of Alkan's latest production, the *25 Préludes* op. 31, as well as the Two Marches op. 26 and 27, is a masterly

combination of perception and bigotry. Praising the Funeral
March as 'the perfect expression of religious fear mingled with
regret' he goes on to challenge several 'unjustifiable harmonic
audacities' in the *Marche Triomphale*. His searching analysis of
these outrages against a harmonic system of which he was
himself the self-appointed guardian makes quaint reading
today. There then follows a very full and enlightened discussion
of the new Preludes. The form, style, atmosphere and even the
interpretation of each piece is considered in turn and Fétis has
only one reservation, the composer's tendency to return again
and again to an atmosphere of melancholy. Indeed he believes
this atmosphere pervades too much of Alkan's work, even the
Marche Triomphale. In seeking an explanation he echoes
Kreutzer's warning: 'When an artist sees himself unappreciated
while others with little talent create reputations, he becomes
irritated: he retires into himself and despises his century. Then,
either he condemns himself to silence, or his work becomes
imbued with a melancholy which only indicates his mournful
state of spirit, not his natural gifts. He continues: 'Alkan is not
just a great pianist, he is an original composer stirred by the
sacred fire. Unfortunately too many years have elapsed and still
his ability has not been recognised for what it is. But is not this
destiny perhaps the artist's own fault? Has he not become
discouraged too soon?' Fétis ends with a plea. 'An artist owes it
to himself, his time and his century to allow his faculties full
rein. God does not grant these gifts without obligation'.

When he uttered these words Fétis was sixty-three, the elder
statesman and spokesman of a generation of French musicians
who had watched Alkan's career unfold from its early promise
to its present uncertainty. He and Kreutzer had sounded Alkan
out and their worst fears were confirmed. These public
expressions of their misgivings, however, although kindly
meant, were probably misplaced and may even have driven the
sensitive artist further in on himself. Certainly Alkan took little
heed of their exhortations. His public career continued to
stagnate while the early promise of a distinguished academic
position had also withered, unfulfilled. When, in 1842, the
seemingly indestructible Cherubini, for twenty years Director
of the Conservatoire, had at last died, Alkan found himself
deprived of one of his earliest benefactors. The appointment

moreover of the celebrated opera composer, Auber, in Cherubini's place was to prove a further check to his faltering career.

Fortunately Alkan's finest creative achievements were often wrested from a background of dark uncertainty and whatever his psychological condition might have been during this disquieting period, he was not idle. In 1847 he published his important *Douze Études dans tous les tons Majeurs*, op. 35 and then, towards the end of the year he unleashed a great monster of a work, the *Grande Sonate* op. 33. Raymond Lewenthal has described this sonata as 'a cosmic event in the composer's development and in the history of piano music'. Its four epic movements, each slower than the last, represent man's psychological state at the ages of 20, 30, 40 and 50. Fétis must have been dismayed by the Finale, a devastatingly powerful Adagio subtitled *Prometheus Bound* in which man suffers his final disintegration. As William Mann has remarked 'It seems that Alkan, at 30 expected to be an old crock at 50'!

The Sonata was dedicated to the composer's father, Alkan Morhange, now sixty-seven, anything but an 'old crock' and still teaching as vigorously as ever. The following advertisement had appeared only three years earlier: 'Monsieur Alkan Père of 12, Rue des Marais-du-Temple, Paris, is taking boarders for music. The numerous successful pupils trained by M. Alkan Père over the last twenty years who have entered the Conservatoire recommend this skilful teacher to the confidence and kindness of families'. (*La France Musicale, 1844*)

6 Marmontel

The publication in 1847 of Alkan's *Grande Sonate* was a landmark in the history of piano music. Not only was the work quite unlike any other sonata but it also opened up a new world of technical possibilities. One can well imagine the composer's hopes and anxieties as he awaited reaction to this latest and most ambitious work. For three years now the Symphony on which he had pinned such high hopes had been lying in his portfolio untried, unheard. His participation in the public musical life of Paris was becoming tenuous in the extreme. One has very much the impression of a man caught between the opposing forces of ambition and retreat, hovering in a kind of no-man's-land of grey uncertainty. He was now in his mid-thirty's. His prestige as a pianist was almost legendary, yet he seemed unable or, perhaps, unwilling to exploit it. On the other hand his experience as a teacher and his unchallenged authority as one of the leading musicians of his day had still not brought him the expected reward of a major post in the Conservatoire, its financial security and the cachet which always attends such a position. If ever an artist needed a moral and psychological boost it was Alkan in 1848. Would not this latest proof of his originality and mastery surely stifle any lingering doubts about his position as the greatest pianist-composer to have emerged from the French school? At the outset of 1848 the work was hardly in print when Paris became plunged in revolution, its artistic life at a standstill. 'All the Parisian pianists are here in London' wrote Chopin, one of the many fugitives from a turbulent city; and so Alkan's *Grande Sonate* was stillborn, unnoticed, unplayed and, like his

Symphony, condemned to oblivion. Not until after the bloodletting of June 1848 was some degree of social life restored to a city still wracked by political instability. By this time, however, Alkan could give little thought to either politics or composition: for the chance he had so long sought seemed at last within his grasp.

During that stifling summer of 1848, with the thunder of violence still menacing a divided capital, a bloodless, but no less bitter struggle for power was in progress within the walls of the Conservatoire itself. Joseph Zimmerman, sensing a mounting hostility from the establishment, decided to relinquish his position as Head of the Piano Department. As Zimmerman's favourite and most distinguished pupil Alkan was, by common consent, the 'heir apparent' to this important post and the moment the vacancy was advertised he put forward his name. He and three other candidates were short-listed. Emile Prudent and Louis Lacombe were no mean pianists but hardly serious competitors against a musician of Alkan's standing. As for the fourth nominee, Alkan must have let out a gasp of astonishment: Antoine Francois Marmontel, his old pupil and camarade. How was it possible that a musician of so little substance, a mere run-of-the-mill product of the Conservatoire could find his name coupled with those of the celebrated Prudent and Lacombe, not to mention that of Alkan himself? Surely he could not be taken seriously by the selection committee?

Even so, the very presence of so unlikely a name as that of Marmontel among the selected candidates, must have caused Alkan a mild twinge of anxiety. A few discreet enquiries soon resolved the mystery. Marmontel was protecting his position by playing up to Auber, the Head of the Conservatoire, and Auber, in turn, was quite clearly favouring Marmontel with his friendship. Anxiety gave way to panic. The reticent Alkan had to act quickly. He could no longer count on Zimmerman who, as the former teacher of all four candidates, could take no part in the nomination of his successor. He found himself alone, fighting not only for his own future but, as he saw it, the whole future standard of teaching in the Conservatoire. It is always an embarrassment to see a man acting out of character but the following letters must be allowed to speak for themselves. Alkan immediately set about obtaining letters of recommendation to be sent to those concerned with the nomination, notably the recently appointed Director of the Department of Fine Arts, Charles Blanc.

Alkan to George Sand. Monday 14th August 1848.
'Excellent Madam,
    I have just read your two letters to my mother and have passed on to M. Ch. Blanc the one that concerns him. If you could have seen my mother's face you would have read on it the expression of thanks you so warmly deserve. I do not yet know what course this affair will take, each day presenting new intrigues, new difficulties: but I tell you quite seriously, whatever happens, I am very happy that it has yielded to me the testimonials with which you honoured me this morning'.

Alkan to George Sand. 23rd August 1848.
    'I did not wish to worry you again about myself, Madam ... but, however indiscreet I may seem, I am so worried I can wait no longer.
    ... My rivals, one above all — the most unworthy — are gaining ground each day. If, amidst all the preoccupations which I appreciate only too well, M. Ch. Blanc were able, and willing to settle this matter immediately and in my favour, he could do so ... I see the 'École' [Conservatoire] threatened by the most unbelievable, the most disgraceful nomination. Two have already been made since the arrival of the new Board at the Department of Fine Arts. I see they are very afraid of making a third mistake, and perhaps their fear, together with bad advice, will make them do just this. Come to my help, Madam, by being willing to make your voice heard to M. Ch. B., however distressing the circumstances may be. Otherwise, M. Auber, who does not like me at all, in returning the friendship of him [Marmontel] who will dishonour the Conservatoire, will regain the ground which a new system of nomination, under which I had some chance, had made him lose, and he will ruin my candidature ... I draw my courage from your last letter.'

Despite George Sand's intervention on his behalf it soon became clear that Alkan's position was becoming eroded still further and on 1st September he decided to write direct to the Home Office (Ministère de L'Intérieur) as well as to Charles Blanc.

'Monsieur le Ministre,
   I have just been told about the words you exchanged with the honourable representatives, Victor Hugo and Donatien Marquis, about the teaching vacancy at the Conservatoire. I have the alternative of seeming a little discourteous, perhaps, or keeping quiet, which would be stupid. Please understand that I am breaking my silence only as a last resort.
   The pupils claimed by M. Marmontel are not his at all. ... For instance Mlle. Malescot, first prize last year, took lessons from Chopin and, moreover Herz ...' A list of similar examples follows and Alkan concludes: 'My heart bleeds, my face is covered in blushes and shame to use such means, but there has never been such a battle between justice and injustice'

To Charles Blanc Alkan pleads time to rally the support of all the leading musicians:

'For example amongst the pianists MM. Liszt, Chopin, Thalberg etc: amongst the critics, MM. Fétis, Berlioz etc: and finally amongst the instrumentalists of every sort, through the most justly famous names in the whole of Europe'.

During the following four days a volley of letters was dispatched, each more desperate than the last:

                                                                    3rd September 1848
'Monsieur le Ministre,
   ... If you sound out the opinion of the public, instead of that of just a small clique, I will be elected.
If you collect the votes of all the leading musicians in Europe, I will be elected.
If you judge the competition on three aspects — performance, composition and teaching — I will be elected ...' etc.

The impression that Alkan was waging a lone battle is a little deceptive. He also had his supporters. The writer, Donatien Marquis, comments on the short list of candidates drawn up by the Director of the Conservatoire:

' ... I am astonished to get the reply that M. Auber had, in fact, mentioned M. Alkan but that he had put his name third on the list: and Marmontel was No. 1. with a very long note giving the greatest possible details to his claims. As for Alkan, the article about him was much shorter. We have replied that we could not help believing that Auber was under some influence, for public sentiment was so opposed to the order he has adopted that the Director of Fine Arts ought to investigate the matter, and it should be easy to arrive at the truth!'

Extracts from a further long letter from Donatien Marquis to a M. Raynal are still more explicit:

'M. Marmontel is quite simply a solfège teacher who was given M. Hertz's class in his absence ... those pupils obliged to follow his course were forced to seek lessons outside the college ... M. Alkan does not owe his reputation to publicity, to flattering women, to an 'Air Varié' on popular tunes ... he loves art for art's sake. He has opposed charlatanism for twenty-three years and has confidence in the justice of mankind ...'

Alkan to George Sand   Friday ? September 1848
'In spite of my positive rights, in spite of your all-powerful support, Madam. I have failed ...
The Republic, for which I have a most ardent love, allows strange blunders to be made. So far as my own sphere is concerned I felt disposed to educate a whole generation in musical matters and I have to give way, not to a worthy or even unworthy rival, but to one of the most total nonentities I can think of ... '

Auber had taken ruthless advantage of the delicate political climate which followed the 1848 Revolution to wield his powerful influence in Marmontel's favour. It was inconceivable that such politically motivated supporters of Alkan as George Sand would dare provoke an open scandal during the tensions of that summer and so the justice in which Alkan so naïvely believed was not forthcoming. As for Marmontel, his reign as

Head of the piano faculty was long and distinguished and was marked in 1858, with further backing from Auber, by the Légion d'Honneur. His pupils included Bizet and he went on to teach the young Debussy just before his retirement in 1887.

In his book *Les Pianistes Célébres* Marmontel goes out of his way to be magnanimous towards Alkan. This is how, just thirty years after the event, he deals with the Conservatoire nomination: 'We are particularly happy to render this public homage to our illustrious colleague [Alkan] for at a certain moment in our careers, in 1848, a most unfortunate misunderstanding, caused by the struggle for Zimmerman's class, separated us without, however, altering our mutual esteem and without diminishing on my part my sincere admiration for the artist; my deep sympathy for the untiring seeker and powerful creator.'

Had Alkan but realised that, for over a century, our main information about him would be from the velvet pen of this man, the irony would have been complete.

M.A. Marmontel
(Artist's realisation from a photograph:
courtesy of Bibliothèque Nationale, *Paris)*

7   Recluse

As Alkan returned to the unproductive routine of private
teaching, his main source of income, he had ample cause to
brood over the harsh reality of his situation. At thirty-five he
had witnessed the triumphs on the one hand and the adulation
on the other of his friends Liszt and Chopin. Their names were
already written in musical history. Although no less
prodigiously gifted as a performer, accomplished as a composer
or amibitious as a teacher his whole style must have lacked
either the sheer autocratic showmanship of a Liszt and a
Paganini or the elusive magic of a Field and a Chopin. Neither
could his bluntly honest attitude to his profession have
commended him to the smooth expediency of the corridors of
power. Like a hammer-blow the Conservatoire deception must
have convinced him that he had waited too long: that even his
friends in high places were unable to supply that final boost, so
indispensable for a career such as his, to ignite.

Alkan may now have had every excuse to take umbrage and
sulk in solitude. Instead, he defied his destiny by inviting five of
the leading Paris string players to join him, on 5th May 1849, in
a public appearance which was to prove his last for nearly
twenty-five years. The programme — utterly uncompromising
and making no concession to public taste — was described in the
press as a 'bold experiment, attempted for the first time, of a
concert comprised exclusively of classics and earlier music'. In
fact, such unpopular novelties as Bach's D minor keyboard
Concerto and Mozart's B flat Sonata for Violin and Piano
formed a framework for Alkan's own compositions: several of
the slighter Préludes and a new *Zorcico* in quintuple time, as

well as the inevitable *Marche Triomphale* into which 'he hurled
all the treasures, all the splendours of rich and grandiose
harmony and all the effects and contrasts of brilliant sonority
...' ... so wrote Henri Blanchard in the *Revue et Gazette*. In his
highly laudatory review he also commented on the rarity of
Alkan's appearances and the distinction of his audience which,
on this occasion, included such artists as Delacroix, Meyerbeer
and Scheffer. Chopin was by now too ill to attend his friend's
concert but as recently as April, the Conservatoire affair still
ringing savagely in Alkan's mind, he, Chopin and Delacroix
had been able to discuss it, the latter noting laconically in his
diary 'by standing up to Auber he [Alkan] has suffered, and
doubtless will continue to suffer, many great annoyances'.

Only too soon Alkan was to sustain a further blow when
Chopin died on 17th October 1849. He was now deprived of the
one friend with whom he had always been able to communicate;
to discuss his personal and artistic problems; whose approach to
his career, whether as composer, performer or teacher had
seemed so similar to his own. Like Chopin, Alkan had found it
lucrative and congenial to give private piano lessons to
fashionable young ladies anxious to boast of a famous teacher
before displaying their accomplishments. Both teachers had
similar methods — the inevitable use of Clementi's *Gradus ad
Parnassum* for instance — and so it is hardly surprising that
Chopin's pupils now turned to his next-door-neighbour as their
master's natural successor. During most of his long life Alkan's
main source of revenue must have come from the teaching of an
aristocratic élite drawn from the fashionable circles of Paris and
including princesses, duchesses and the wives of distinguished
diplomats. We have no information about the amount of
teaching he did nor how much he charged but if it was
comparable to Chopin's exceptional fee of twenty francs a lesson
he was at least spared financial worry for the next few years.

Soon after the death of Chopin further professional links were
severed when Alkan moved away from the still famous artistic
colony in the Square d'Orléans and from now on his
appearances at public gatherings became increasingly rare.
Between 1849 and 1853 he was occasionally seen at the first
night of a few of George Sand's plays. Thanking her for his
ticket for *Francois-le-Champi* on 23rd November 1849, he

Très-excellente Madame,
si d'aventure vous deviez
être à Paris et si vous
y trouvant, vous vouliez
bien venir à ma petite
soirée du 23, ce me serait
un bien grand honneur,
et un plaisir plus
grand encore.

C. V. Alkan
aîné

11 r: La Bruyère

10/4/ 53

A note from Alkan to George Sand

wrote: 'Your note and the performance cured my misanthropy
... I felt my shrunken heart expand'.

Other letters of the period hint at the occasional soirée when
Alkan played to a small gathering, but soon even these fitful
efforts to keep in touch were abandoned. Unpredictable,
moody and increasingly worried about his personal health,
Alkan was fast becoming a recluse. Those friends who
attempted to drag him from his shell were liable to strange
rebuffs. To a kindly invitation from Ambroise Thomas he
replied: 'Even if I were to indulge myself for an hour and a
quarter you would be obliged to carry me off to the infirmary',
while George Sand received the following singular note: 'Thank
you for your kind, affectionate letter, dear Madam, but it seems
that on no account must I have the pleasure of playing for you
this evening because about an hour ago I decided that the music
in question could not take place'.

As Alkan approached forty his physical condition was fast
becoming a morbid and constant preoccupation and his stock
excuse for public inactivity. The extent to which his malady was
imaginaire is debatable. Probably his constitution was never
robust and his clinical faddiness about his diet suggests a poor
digestion. No one was allowed near his food which he would
prepare himself from his own purchases. One of his maids
would refer to her master's invariable and twice cooked diet as
'La ratatouille de Monsieur'.

Early in 1855 the following little note appeared in the *Revue
et Gazette* dated January 7: 'M. Alkan Morhange, head of a
family which has yielded several distinguished artists amongst
whom M. Valentin Alkan, the famous pianist, is first and
foremost, has just died aged seventy-five.'

From the mid 1850's Alkan's withdrawal from social life was
complete. Only his pupils were admitted at their appointed
hour and although it has sometimes been hinted that certain
distinguished visitors to Paris, Liszt in particular, would always
drop in on their old friend, there seems no real evidence of this.
As for others, they were invariably confronted by the concierge
with : 'M. Alkan is not at home'. Even the fleeting mention of his
name in the press would now always refer to his inexplicable
silence: a silence which was only once broken. This isolated
exception must, by its very nature, remain an occasion for

curiosity and conjecture and one which raises the whole question of the composer's exact relationship with the piano manufacturing firm of Erard. At the International Exhibition of 1855, the year in which his father had died, Alkan was very much in evidence demonstrating the company's latest instruments only to return once more to that obscurity which had now become his way of life.

Apart from his absence from the Paris musical scene Alkan's silence as a creative artist was also becoming ominous. Following the publication in 1847 of the *Grande Sonate* nothing of importance had appeared for nearly a decade. His reputation as a composer still rested on a shallow salon piece, the celebrated *Saltarelle*, which had by now become the inevitable concluding item in every other young French pianist's repertoire and was quickly wearing itself to death. Meanwhile Alkan's splendid *Etudes Majeurs*, op. 35 remained unplayed while his orchestral symphony and *Grande Sonate* had glided gently into oblivion: no great incentive one might assume for a serious and controversial composer unable, or unwilling to promote his own work. Moreover Alkan believed himself to be chronically ill and might well have felt every excuse for remaining inactive; but he was also unpredictable and as capable as ever of springing a surprise. Suddenly, in 1857, the floodgates opened and posterity's debt to Auber was made manifest. A mighty avalanche of important piano works brought out during this *Annus Mirabilis* by the publisher, Richault, supplies all the evidence for Alkan's activity during the lost decade which had followed his rejection by the Conservatoire. Neither warning nor reaction accompanied this imposing release yet it included his most famous work, the *Douze études dans tous les tons mineurs*, op. 39. The two hundred and seventy-seven pages of this masterpiece, which included the Solo Symphony and Solo Concerto as well as the brilliant *Festin d'Esope,* would alone, have provided ample proof that Alkan's withdrawal had been more than justified.

Hardly less remarkable, and more immediately accessible however, is a shoal of smaller compositions which accompanied this historic publication. The two sets of *Chants* op. 38, for instance, pay tribute to Mendelssohn's *Songs Without Words* but in a variety of characteristic and sometimes disturbing ways.

Mendelssohn's original key sequence is adopted and the style of each piece is easily recognisable but seen, as it were, in a distorting mirror, enlarged, broadened or darkened in mood and in one case afflicted by the obsessional repetition of an unresolved foreign note within the texture. The laconic *Minuetto alla Tedesca*, three fine Marches, in turn sprightly, powerful or grotesque and the extraordinary *Trois Petites Fantasies* op. 41, all date from this period. This last work is particularly admired in France for its wry and whimsical humour. Prokofiev himself could hardly have surpassed the rhythmic fury of a final, fulgurating toccata in which Alkan deals surprise upon surprise for all the world like some master card-sharper in whose hand every card becomes an ace ... not at all, one would have thought, the composition of a self-admitted misanthrope! Three further Marches, op, 40, this time for four hands, also display a growing preoccupation with the humorous, the caricatural and the bizarre. These are dedicated to his old friend Hiller, director of the Conservatorium at Cologne.

Writing to Hiller in 1857 Alkan regrets the distance that prevents his trying out the new Marches with his friend. He complains once more of his ill-health: 'I give lessons during the day' he writes 'while in the evening, during those few moments of lucidity, spared me by my illness, I am correcting the proofs of my new Sonata for piano and basse ('cello) which I am having printed myself. (*sic*) I would so much like to play this at Erard's but my poor health prevents it. Still more would I love to play it to you but this is unlikely for, like me you are preoccupied with trying to make ends meet. I only just manage to scrape a wretched living and I haven't, like you, the responsibility of a wife and family'.

Ferdinand Hiller (1810-1885) is remembered not only as the dedicatee of the Schumann Piano Concerto and the teacher of Max Bruch but also as the youthful witness of a famous death-bed reconciliation; that of his master, Hummel with the dying Beethoven. Hiller had lived in Paris from 1828-1835 and had given the first performances there of some of the greatest keyboard works of Bach and Beethoven, including the *Emperor Concerto*. His authoritative ·playing had won him the admiration and friendship of every musician of note from

Cherubini to Berlioz, Liszt, Chopin and, of course, Alkan himself. Later he had returned to his native Germany where he was now making a great mark as a conductor. From the mid-1850's Hiller and Alkan corresponded regularly and the exciting discovery in Cologne of seventy-three letters written by Alkan to his friend, and spanning a period of over thirty years, throws an invaluable light on his tastes and passions, his psychological condition, his domestic problems and even his barbed humour. Indeed it soon becomes clear that Hiller must have filled the gap once occupied by Chopin as the one person in whom he could confide and discuss his problems. Certainly Hiller was one of the few visitors to Paris to whom Alkan was always 'at home' ... except on one occasion which misfired. Hearing the door-bell Alkan hastily sent his servant with the stock plea 'Not at home'. Almost at once he recognised his friend's card and realising his gaffe rushed from the house, but just too late to greet Hiller. Alkan's embarrassment and dismay at missing him is captured in a series of quite desperate notes to various likely addresses attempting to explain, apologise and arrange a rendezvous.

8   Prometheus Bound

Despite constant misgivings about his health Alkan had, by 1857, come to terms with a mode of existence quietly divorced from the reassurance of either professional approval or public acclaim. Wealthy pupils, like the Princess Orloff, provided him with sufficient income for his modest tastes and left him enough time for creative work and for what his friend Hiller humorously called his 'semitic studies'. These included translating the Bible, two or three verses regularly each day, and by 1858 he was claiming to have completed three-quarters of the entire work. In 1865 Alkan was translating the New Testament from the Syriac, and the Bible remained his constant inspiration, spilling over into several of his compositions. Like the Adagio of his lost Symphony the wonderful slow movement of the 'Cello Sonata op. 47 is prefaced by a few lines from the Old Testament and his piano composition *Super Flumina Babylonis* op. 52 is a kind of wordless operatic scena paraphrasing Psalm 137. 'If only I could have my life over again' he once declared 'I would set the entire Bible to music'.

Other reading in 1858 included the famous treatise on orchestration by Berlioz. Alkan deeply admired Berlioz's orchestral genius but not his music which he associated with the new school of Wagner and Liszt of which he heartily disapproved. His opinion of Berlioz as a writer is succinctly expressed: 'It is always a revelation for me to read that man for alongside interesting and amusing things one comes across utter drivel'.

It speaks highly of the feverish excitement generated by Wagner's presence in Paris at the outset of 1860 that Alkan was

reluctantly persuaded to attend the first concert in which
Wagner conducted his own compositions in the 'Théâtre des
Italiens' on January 25th, an event that caught Paris by the
throat and split the musical élite. Alkan sought refuge in the
interval excusing himself, with an ironic smile and complaining
that it was 'far too noisy'. He later commented 'Wagner is not
music; it's a sickness'.

Although taking no personal part in the musical life of the
capital he would still cast a quizzical eye at the various
celebrities who came and went, especially the pianists. He
admired Anton Rubinstein: 'marvellous technique' — that was
also in 1860 — but thought he took himself too seriously as a
composer. Doubtless, had Rubinstein known this he would not
have dedicated his 5th Piano Concerto to Alkan. He also heard
but did not see 'the illustrious Madame Schumann'. Writing to
Hiller in May 1862 Alkan admitted that although his view of the
lady had been unfortunately obscured by a pillar, she had given
him considerable pleasure ... 'that is, for a woman'. 'These days'
he added 'I see so few people that I have no idea of the
impression she has made in Paris, but I have a hunch her
admirers overrate her', and then as an afterthought: 'I hope you
won't be affronted by my judgment of the excellent Madame
Schumann — it's really more a matter of personal
temperament. For my taste women never play really well. Either
they sound like women or they try and sound like men'.

Such isolated excursions apart, Alkan was now an almost
total recluse. 'He locks away his talent as singlemindedly as
others in his place would seek to exploit it' wrote a leading
periodical in 1860 and a year later a mutual acquaintance was
warning Hiller: 'Alkan has now taken refuge in the most
complete obscurity'. Even so his retirement from public life
seemed to have quickened his interest in public affairs and in
1859 he was writing detailed letters to Hiller fervently defending
the French position over Napoléon 3rd's latest military
adventure, the Franco-Italian campaign against the Austrians.
Alkan's deeper concern for the shallow glory and grim futility of
war is reserved for the graphically simple but psychologically
complex *Military Caprices* op. 50 of that year.

One of Alkan's most overtly freakish works also dates from
1859, his *Funeral March for a Dead Parrot*, scored for three

oboes, bassoon and mixed voices. One may reasonably infer that 'Jacko', deceased hero of this grotesque study in mock pathos, had been a recent member of the establishment: an establishment that clearly afforded Alkan the right degree of stability for creative work. The quaintly neo-classical *Minuets* op. 51 of 1859, the Forty-Eight *Esquisses* op. 63 and the masterly *Sonatine* of 1861 op. 61, all reveal a sharper, at times even abrasive edge to Alkan's pen. Indeed, it is remarkable, given so little encouragement and plagued by ill-health, whether real or imaginary, that he was able for a further four years to sustain the creative peak he had so obviously reached with the op. 39 Studies. The harvest might well have continued but during the summer of 1861 his housekeeper left after looking after his establishment, if not his *cuisine*, for over fifteen years.

   Alkan was now in real trouble. Before the end of the year he had rejected fifty-one maids and was still alone. 'Have you ever made your own bed, my dear Hiller?' he wrote. 'I'm becoming daily more and more misanthropic and misogynous ... nothing worthwhile, good or useful to do ... no one to devote myself to. My situation makes me horridly sad and wretched. Even musical production has lost its attraction for me for I can't see the point or goal ... But, enough of my moral infirmities and a thousand pardons for boring you with them'. Ironically enough Alkan might easily have received just that distraction from his moral infirmities he so vitally needed by reading a most enthusiastic article which had appeared in the *Neue Berliner Musikzeiten* about his *Studies* op. 35 by Liszt's son-in-law, Hans von Bulow. Alkan received this article but gave it to someone to translate who promptly lost it.

   To add to his worries he was now obliged to look for a new flat. His constant anxiety about the high cost of living and the danger of having to suffocate himself with too much teaching suggests that several moves in the late 1850's and early '60's were forced on him by financial considerations. In 1863 he was still searching in vain for a flat within his means. Time was running out and he was even considering selling everything and taking a single room in the Latin Quarter where he would divide his life equally between study, preparing his food and doing his own chores. It is impossible to judge the extent to which Alkan liked to exaggerate his physical, financial and 'moral' infirmities. He could certainly not have been destitute for he did eventually find himself suitable accommodation in a fashionable part of Paris. By November 1863 he was established in the Rue de la Croix-du-Roule which, in 1869, changed its name to the Rue Daru and here he was to remain for the rest of his life.

* * * * * *

During the 1860's the long-established 'Concerts du Conservatoire' were being sharply challenged by a new series of 'Concerts Populaires' which took place each Sunday afternoon at exactly the same hour. By 1864 Alkan had not taken part in a public concert for fifteen years and he was somewhat taken aback to receive an engagement from Hainl, the recently appointed conductor of the Conservatoire orchestra, to appear as soloist at one of these famous concerts. Hardly had Alkan recovered from his surprise when there came another invitation, this time from Pasdeloup, the enterprising young conductor of the 'Concerts Populaires'. Would Alkan like to submit an orchestral composition to be brought forward during the coming season? Alkan's *B Minor Symphony* had by now been gathering dust for two decades. Was there, perhaps, a concerted effort to entice the shy artist out of his shell? Despite his long silence there must have remained a lingering curiosity among those who had actually heard him and others to whom he was little more than a vague legend. Perhaps the influential Fétis, the dedicatee of Alkan's great *Studies* op. 35 and 39 had whispered in the right ear. If so he had acted too late. Alkan firmly declined both invitations explaining that his present frame of mind would no more allow him to confront the symphonic public as a composer than his health would permit his undertaking to appear on a fixed day at a fixed hour; and he returned to translating the Bible, except when he was unable to write. During the severe winter of 1865 the cold cracked open his finger tips, which seems to indicate an inadequate diet.

Alkan was over fifty, the final age of disintegration he had so graphically prophesied in his *Grande Sonate* of just seventeen years earlier. In his letters he now refers constantly to his 'old age' and to the consolation to be found in religious studies. Of his compositions there is never a hint. His final creative period, approximately from the early '60's to the early '70's contains three further sets of *Chants* and a large number of finely wrought transcriptions. Otherwise his later compositions, like the thirteen *Prières* op. 64 and the *Eleven Grands Préludes* op. 66 show an ever-increasing preoccupation with religious subjects and with the *pédalier*, a normal piano with pedal-board attached. Alkan's wizardry on this hybrid instrument must have been awe-inspiring. Several other French musicians followed in his footsteps, notably Saint-Saëns and, of course, Delaborde, who created a deep impression when he introduced several of 'his master's' latest works for *pédalier* in the Hanover Square Rooms, London, in 1871. Despite the advocacy, however, of a small nucleus of French musicians, the *pédalier* never really caught on outside France and was soon forgotten, as, inevitably was much of the finest of Alkan's later work, which can only make its right effect on this now obsolete instrument.

If Alkan was reluctant to speak about his latest compositions, his letters often provide a sardonic slant on the musical world at large, especially when his literary style reflects some of that barbed subtlety so familiar in his music.

'What do you make of this latest development in our old friend Liszt's career?' he asked Hiller. This was in 1865. Liszt was in Rome, a guest of the Vatican. On April 25 that year, he had become an Abbé and thenceforth wore the Abbé's frock. Alkan seems highly sceptical about the sincerity of Liszt's 'conversion': 'For my part,' he comments, 'should I ever decide to become a Rabbi it would not be for the sake of high office in the Synagogue but rather would I wear the frock with disinterest' adding shrewdly ... 'if Paris was worth a mass perhaps a position at St. Peter's is worth a cassock'.*

As the decade was drawing to a close Alkan's letters began to take on a new and significant turn. 'Old age', 'illness', 'moral infirmities' ... even his 'semitic studies' give way to a re-awakening interest in performing problems. On 1st April

---

*In 1593, when the opportunist Henri IV of France re-united his people by turning Catholic, he is said to have remarked 'Paris is worth a mass'.

1869 he expresses concern about the debatable 'return' in the First Movement of Beethoven's *Hammerklavier* Sonata. Has he and everyone he has ever heard play the work, he asks Hiller, mis-read the two preceding bars as 'A naturals' when, in fact, they are 'sharps' in the signature? Only four days later he is asking his friend about the possibility and style of cadenzas in the Adagio of Bach's Triple Concerto in C* and in the same letter, requests the manuscript of Hiller's own early Trio in F sharp minor adding: 'I feel I would like to appear in public again'.

Why should Alkan, having sheltered these last twenty years under the cloak of ill-health suddenly get the urge to give concerts? Is there, perhaps, a more plausible explanation than the naive assumption that his health had suddenly taken a turn for the better? Apart from the Bible, Alkan had three passions in life; composing, playing and teaching and the importance of the latter to Alkan should not be underestimated. Had not the Conservatoire intrigue robbed him of the opportunity 'to educate a whole generation in musical matters'? Had not his last concerts back in the 1840's taken on more and more an educational as well as artistic function? Could it be that by the late 1869's Alkan found his creativity on the wane and realised that his final mission in life was to perform and introduce those great works he had studied but which were still virtually

---

*Alkan had heard an account of a performance in London of this Concerto in which Mendelssohn, Moscheles and Thalberg improvised cadenzas: but he was misled. S.S. Stratton (*Mendelssohn: The Master Musicians*. Dent 1901) quotes an eye-witness account of this extraordinary performance which took place in 1844 in the Hanover Square Rooms. According to Charles Horsley the work was the Bach Triple Concerto in D minor, not the C major, and the three cadenzas were improvised in the Finale. Mendelssohn's cadenza, the last, he tells us, exploded in a veritable storm of double octaves which sustained its climax for a full five minutes (sic) bringing to a conclusion 'an exhibition of mechanical skill and most perfect inspiration, which, neither before nor since that memorable Thursday afternoon has ever been approached. The effect on the audience was electric'. Mendelssohn later remarked 'I thought the people might like some octaves so I played them'.

Strange to relate there is no place for improvised cadenzas in the D minor Concerto while in the C major they are written out in full, forming an essential part of the fabric and accompanied by orchestra. Music must have been fun in those days!
—

unknown in France? In this way, perhaps, he would not be finally denied the chance to educate a generation. Before Alkan's dream could be realised, however, other and alien events were afoot, and of such magnitude that anything less than the most firmly conceived resolution would have been irrevocably crushed.

* * * * * *

In the summer of 1870 Napoléon 3rd launched his final, disastrous military fling, and within weeks, his armies routed and capitulating to the Prussians, had fled to England. On September 4 a Republic was declared in France, but despite the improvisation of new armies the Prussians had, by September 23 reached Paris. Inevitably France was forced to surrender but not before the besieged capital, with its two million inhabitants, had been subjected to four months of constant bombardment, famine and disease, exacerbated by one of the severest winters of the century. Worse was to follow. Humiliated and stripped of their Eastern provinces the French now started a campaign of self-destruction and by May 1871, Paris was convulsed by a hideous orgy of carnage in which 20,000 perished, many of the finest buildings were burnt and, incidentally, vital official documents relating to the Alkan-Morhange family were lost.

How did Alkan fare during these months of tribulation in which food became so desperately short that cats sold at six francs a carcase, dogs at one franc a pound while, for the less squeamish, there was a thriving black market in rats at a mere one franc each? Once peace was restored he wrote to Hiller, himself a German: 'For forty-nine days and nights without respite I have been living in the midst of cannon balls and bullets. All I have is a shutter and a piano with a hole through them. I have hardly eaten at all'. Even Alkan's fervent patriotism had been tested beyond endurance and his dilemma, like that of so many artists in times of stress, is summed up in his own words: 'Do I renounce my friends because they are Prussian?' ... and he added grimly 'I no longer feel French: only old age'.

Miraculously enough, the heart-searching experience of the Siege of Paris seemed only to have strengthened Alkan's resolve to play in public again. Once more he was pestering the life out of Hiller for the score of his friend's early F sharp minor Trio. 'I would like to play this in Paris next season' he writes, adding enigmatically: 'Delaborde must be told nothing about it' ... and, singularly enough, this is the one solitary mention of Delaborde's name in the whole of this voluminous correspondence which spans three decades.

At the outset of 1873 the Paris musical world must have read with mingled wonder and curiosity the following paragraph in the *Revue et Gazette:* 'Ch.-Valentin Alkan, the eminent pianist and composer who has condemned himself to retirement for too long, returns to the fore with the announcement, which will be received with great interest, of six 'Petits Concerts' of classical music, devoted to compositions of every school and period for piano solo or duet, for *pédalier* or for piano together with other instruments. These performances will take place on the Saturdays of Feb 15, March 1, 15 and 29 and April 12 and 26 at 9.00 p.m. precisely, at the Salle Erard.'

9 Les Petits Concerts

On Saturday evening February 15, 1873 Charles-Valentin Alkan stepped on to the podium at the Salle Erard. It was his first public appearance for nearly a quarter of a century. The programme was formidable. It spared neither audience nor artist and considering the circumstances, and the fact that Alkan, now in his sixtieth year played from memory throughout, it must have taxed him to the limit of his capacity. The following review well captures some of the electricity in the air: 'After a silence of twenty years Ch.-Valentin Alkan, one of the masters of the piano, has made a reappearance. His great talent has remained unchanged ... restrained, learned, accurate ... although he seems to have lost a little of his technique. Moreover, the whole atmosphere, which was if anything still more highly charged than a début, seemed to paralyse the eminent artist at this, his first 'Petit Concert' and was undoubtably responsible for two unfortunate memory lapses, in a study by Stephen Hiller (*sic*) and in the *F major Toccata* by Bach. Alkan also played the *Sonata* op. 110 by Beethoven, three pieces by Rameau, the Allegro from a Concerto by Handel, several studies by Chopin and Hiller and some of his own compositions which are remarkable in every way: a March for Four Hands (with E.M. Delaborde) the first piece from his *Premier recueil de Chants* and the Prière *Deus Sabbaoth*. He still plays the *pédalier* with assurance and perfect clarity as of old. To end the performance he was joined by Alard in the *Introduction and Rondo*, op. 70, by Schubert. The audience, consisting largely of artists, gave the virtuoso and composer one of those warm ovations one never forgets'.

SALONS ÉRARD; 13, RUE DU MAIL.

TROISIÈME ANNÉE.

SIX PETITS CONCERTS DE MUSIQUE CLASSIQUE,

PIANO SEUL, A 2 & A 4 MAINS;
PIANO CONCERTANT, OU AVEC ACCOMPAGNEMENT.
& PIANO A CLAVIER DE PÉDALES; *

DONNÉS PAR M.

CH. Vᵗᵉ ALKAN aîné,

LES VENDREDIS SOIRS : 19 FÉVRIER; 5 ET 19 MARS; 2, 16 ET 30 AVRIL. 1875, A 9 HEURES *très-précises.*

* *Cembalo a Pedale;* **Pedal-Flügel.**

PROGRAMMES : **

PROGRAMME I.

Première Partie

I. LA FINE MADELON, etc., Pieces de	COUPERIN.	(1668-1733.)
II. VIVACE, de	D. SCARLATTI.	(1683-1757.)
III. LES SAUVAGES, de	RAMEAU.	(1683-1764.)
IV. ADAGIO, d'un CONCERTO, pour Clavecin, de	HANDEL.	(1684-1759.)
V. 1ᵉʳ MOUVEMENT, de la 6ᵉ SONATE de	J. S. BACH.	(1685-1750.)
VI. POLONAISES, de	FRIEDMANN BACH.	(1710-1784.)

Premier Intermède :

A. Nᵒ 1. du 1ᵉʳ RECUEIL de CHANTS, pour Piano : } CH : Vᵗᵉ ALKAN.
B. Nᵒ du 4 RECUEIL id : ibid.

Deuxième Partie :

I. Nᵒ 61, du GRADUS, de	CLEMENTI.	(1752-1832.)
II. 1ᵉʳ MORCEAU de SONATE, de	MOZART.	(1756-1791.)
III. LARGO, de l'œu 10 de	BEETHOVEN.	(1770-1827.)
IV. ÉTUDE, en Mib sol mineur, de	MOSCHELES.	(1794-1870.)
V. ROMANCE en Mi bemol, de	FIELD.	(1782-1837.)
VI. SCHERZO, en La bemol, de	WEBER.	(1786-1826.)

Deuxième Intermède :

A. MARCHE des GRANDS-PRÊTRES, de l'ALCESTE; et } GLUCK.
B. CHŒUR des SCYTHES, de l'IPHIGENIE EN TAURIDE : avec Clavier de Pédales obligé.

Troisième Partie :

I. PRESTISSIMO, de l'œu 7, de	CZERNY.	(1791-1857.)
II. PENSÉE MUSICALE, de	SCHUBERT.	(1797-1828.)
III. 2ᵉ POLONAISE, de l'œu 26, de	KESSLER.	(1800-1872.)
IV. ÉTUDE, en Fa min : de	MENDELSSOHN.	(1809-1847.)
V. POLONAISE, de l'œu 26, de	CHOPIN.	(1810-1849.)
VI. FANTAISIE, de l'œu 111, de	SCHUMANN.	(1810-1856.)

PROGRAMME II.

Première Partie :

I. SONATE, œu : 78, de	SCHUBERT.
II. FANTASIA; op : 77, de	BEETHOVEN.
III. POLONAISE, en Mi bemol, de	WEBER.

Intermède :

A. DEUX MORCEAUX RELIGIEUX pour Piano à Clavier de Pédales : } CH : Vᵗᵉ ALKAN.
B. 3 NUMÉROS des 48 MOTETS, pour Piano seul, de . . HANDEL.
C. UNE TRANSCRIPTION, du SAMSON, de :

Deuxième Partie :

I. FANTAISIES, pour Clarinette et Piano; œu : 73, de :	SCHUMANN.
II. PRÉLUDE, ADAGIO et PASTORALE, pour Piano à Clavier de Pédales, de :	J : S : BACH.
III. FANTAISIE, en La min :, de :	MENDELSSOHN.

PROGRAMME III.

Première Partie :

I. SONATE; œu : 110, de	BEETHOVEN.
II. PRIÈRE PENDANT LA BATAILLE; Chant et Piano :	WEBER.
III. CHORAL, et FUGUE en Ré, pour Piano à Clavier de Pédales, de :	J : S : BACH.

Intermède :

Duo, pour Piano et Violoncelle. . . . . CHOPIN.

Deuxième Partie :

I. DEUX PRÉLUDES de l'œuvre 28, de	J : S : BACH.
II. RÉCITATIF, et AIR, pour Voix de Basse et Cembalo obligato, de	
III. MENUET, et 3ᵉ POLONAISE, de l'œu : 25; pour Piano à Clavier de Pédales :	HANDEL, & KESSLER.

PROGRAMME IV.

Première Partie :

I. TRIO, pour Piano, Violon et Violoncelle, de :	MOZART.
II. CHŒUR de l'OBERON, transcrit pour Piano à Clavier de Pédales :	WEBER.
III. DEUXIEME SONATE, de	CHOPIN.

Intermède :

A. IMPROMPTU . . .
B. MARCHE FUNEBRE . . . . . . } CH : Vᵗᵉ ALKAN.
C. MENUET SYMPHONIQUE . . . .
D. FANTAISIE, pour deux Pianos à Clavier de Pédales : SAINT-SAËNS.

Deuxième Partie :

I. SONATA, pour Piano et Violon, de :	J : S : BACH.
II. MAZURKA, et 1ʳᵉ BALLADE, de :	CHOPIN.
III. DEUX TRANSCRIPTIONS, pour Piano; de l'ARMIDE, et de la SYMPHONIE en Mi bemol, de :	GLUCK. & MOZART.

PROGRAMME V.

Première Partie :

I. A. CHORAL, et : } BACH, & SCHUMANN.
B. CANON, pour Piano à Clavier de Pédales, de :
II. SONATE; op : 109, de . . . . BEETHOVEN.
III. A. CHORAL, et : } BACH, & HANDEL.
B. VARIATIONS, pour Piano à Pédales; de :

Intermède :

A. PRÉLUDE VI, pour Piano à Pédales :
B. *La Chanson de la bonne Vieille....* du 4ᵉ RECUEIL de CHANTS pour Piano : } CH : Vᵗᵉ ALKAN.
C. L'ÉTUDE en Ut dièse, avec accompagnement d'Orchestre :

Deuxième Partie :

I. CONCERTO, en Si min : avec accompagnement d'Orchestre; œu : 89, de :	HUMMEL.
II. MENUETS, de	RAMEAU.
III. A. CHORAL, et : } BACH, & HAYDN.	
B. ANDANTE, pour Piano à Pédales, de :	

PROGRAMME VI.

Première Partie :

I. SONATE, à 4 Mains, de :	MOZART.
II. DEUX TRANSCRIPTIONS pour Piano à Clavier de Pédales, de :	WEBER, & J : S : BACH.
III. PRÉLUDE, et FUGUE V; de :	MENDELSSOHN.

Intermède :

I. MARCHES, à 4 Mains; et } CH : Vᵗᵉ ALKAN.
II. SONATE, pour Piano et Violon :

Deuxième Partie :

I. MAZURKA, et 8ᵉ BALLADE, de :	CHOPIN.
II. ROMANCE SANS PAROLES, de :	MENDELSSOHN.
III. CHORAL, et FUGUE, en Sol; pour Piano à Pédales, de :	J : S : BACH.

** Des Affiches et des Programmes, Ultérieurs et Spéciaux, donneront, pour chacun des Six Petits Concerts, les Indications complémentaires de la plupart des Ouvrages exécutés; ainsi que les Noms des Artistes qui se feront entendre dans les Morceaux Concertants, etc.

On pourra se procurer à l'avance des Billets, Simples ou d'Abonnement, aux Adresses suivantes :
MM. BRANDUS et Cⁱᵉ, Éditeurs de Musique, 103, rue de Richelieu ;
DURAND, SCHŒNEWERK et Cⁱᵉ, Éditeurs, 4, Place de la Madeleine ;
M. E. GIROD, Éditeur, 16, Boulevard Montmartre ;
Et Maison ÉRARD, 13, Rue du Mail.

Prix du Billet (numéroté) : **6 francs.**
Abonnement, pour les Six Séances : 30 francs.

IMPRIMERIE CENTRALE DES CHEMINS DE FER. — A. CHAIX ET Cⁱᵉ, RUE BERGÈRE, 20, A PARIS. — 11054-4.

Although encouraged by his reception Alkan was deeply exercised by this newly discovered tendency to stage fright. Only two weeks separated him from his next encounter with a sophisticated public: something had to be done, and quickly. Since his youth a salon had always been placed at his disposal in the Maison Erard, and realising that his nervousness could be simply a matter of rehabilitation, of acclimatising himself once more to the disturbing presence of an audience, he decided to give an informal recital there twice a week. From now on acquaintances and their friends could drop in at Erard's any Monday or Thursday afternoon and hear Alkan range spontaneously throughout his vast repertoire or give an impromptu preview of an impending concert. This discipline evidently paid off for at his second 'Petit Concert' on March 1 he found his old form. Unabashed by his recent, unhappy experience he ran the gauntlet once more of Bach's *F major Toccata*, this time with impunity, and Delaborde and another pianist joined with him in a performance of Bach's *Triple Concerto in C* (presumably Alkan had solved the problem of cadenzas) and among a group of his own compositions he included the early *Study in C sharp* with string accompaniment which still remained one of his favourite party pieces. This time the review was unequivocal: 'The eminent composer, the noble, austere pianist, the masterly *pédalier*-player was acclaimed by a public of connoisseurs, the public of great artists'. So, it seems, Alkan still played, as he always had for an élite. At no time are we told the size of the audience at the 'Petits Concerts', only of its quality.

The organisation of these concerts was taken in hand by Alkan's youngest brother, Gustave, who seems to have inherited some of his father's business flair. He master-minded the whole enterprise from booking the hall and dealing with the publicity, to numbering the seats and supervising the audience during the performances. Alkan himself, of course, devised the programmes and, although prepared to consider the layout with a few intimate friends, he was quite dictatorial about their content. One of these friends was Alexandre de Bertha who first met the composer at a time when the concerts were still being planned. He assures us that Alkan was never above discussing the problems of interpretation of the music he was about to

SALONS ÉRARD: 13, RUE DU MAIL.

30 Avril 1874.

à **9** heures *très-précises.*

PROGRAMME VI.

DES

SIX PETITS CONCERTS

DE

M. CH : Vᵗᵉ ALKAN aîné.

(DEUXIÈME ANNÉE.)

	Durée approximative des Numéros.
PREMIÈRE PARTIE :	
I. **Quintetto**. en *Mi bémol*. pour Hautbois. Clarinette. Cor. Basson et Piano : . . . . **MOZART.**	I. *a.* 9 à 10 Min. *b.* 7 à 8 Min. *c.* 5 à 6 Min.
a **Largo** et **Allegro moderato**; *b.* **Larghetto**; *c.* **Allegretto** : Exécuté avec **MM. LALLIET. GRISEZ. DUPONT** et **ESPAIGNET.**	
II. *a.* **Nocturne**. en *Ut min*. (Moderato espressivo ;) . . . . **FIELD.**	II. *a.* 3 Minutes.
b. **Nocturne**. également en *Ut min*. : Nᵒ 1, de l'œuv : 48 : (Lento) . . **CHOPIN.**	*b.* 6 Minutes.
III. **Menuet**. en *Trio*, et **Passacaille**. pour Piano à Clavier de Pédales. . **HÆNDEL.**	III. *a.* 2 Minutes. *b.* 5 à 6 Min.
INTERMÈDE :	
Duo. pour Piano et Violon, op : 21 :	
a. Assez animé.	*a.* 6 Minutes.
b. Lentement. — **L'Enfer.** — } CH : Vᵗᵉ **ALKAN.**	*b.* 4 Minutes.
c. Vivacissime.	*c.* 9 Minutes.
Exécuté avec **M. LÉONARD.**	
DEUXIÈME PARTIE :	
I. **Larghetto**, en *Mi*, du **1ᵉʳ Concerto**; op : 11, de : . . . . **CHOPIN.**	I. 6 à 7 Minutes.
II. **Les Nonnettes :** — **Les Blondes et les Brunes :** — Nᵒ 13, du Fr : **COUPERIN** 1ᵉʳ Livre, des **Pièces** de Clavecin, de : . . . .) (DIT LE GRAND.)	II. 2 Minutes.
III. *a.* **Choral :**	III. *a.* 2 Minutes.
« Ich raf' su dir, Herr Jesus-Christ : » . . . . } J : S : **BACH.**	*b.* 8 Minutes.
b. **Toccata**. en *Fa*, pour Piano à Pédales.	

IMPRIMERIE CENTRALE DES CHEMINS DE FER. — A. CHAIX ET Cⁱᵉ. RUE BERGÈRE. 20. A PARIS. — 5192-1.

play: 'It was thus that I came to understand the immense
horizon of his musical knowledge' he writes, adding that not
only was Alkan conversant with every school of the past, but that
his extraordinary memory found no difficulty in dredging up
works he had not encountered since his youth. So far as his
contemporaries were concerned he was severely selective. Liszt
and his school held no fascination for Alkan who reserved his
enthusiasm for composers like Weber, Mendelssohn,
Schumann and Chopin, who had not entirely broken with
classical tradition. Add to this his insatiable exploration of the
German classics, both as an original subscriber to the *Bach
Gesellschaft* and as an impassioned apostle of late Beethoven,
and the framework of his programmes becomes inevitable.

As well as devising his programmes Alkan was also
responsible for setting them out in the utmost detail down to the
quaintly fastidious timing of each piece or movement, an
innovation prompted by the advantage to concert-goers of
indicating in advance when their carriages should arrive, but
one which has apparently not outlived the *pédalier*.

Once established, a series of 'Six Petits Concerts' was given
each season for the next five years with a break in 1876 caused by
alterations to the Salle Erard. Apart from Delaborde and
Alard, such celebrities as Saint-Saëns, his old friend
Franchomme and the famous Madame Viardot all took part.
Tantalisingly enough, not one of those major piano works on
which Alkan's reputation now rests was included, complete.
Thus, during the first season he played exerpts from his great
Solo Concerto and the following year the Funeral March and
Minuet only from his *Solo Symphony*. Instinctively, it seems,
Alkan had always feared that these gigantic works would be
misunderstood even by his own reasonably sophisticated
audiences. There was also, perhaps, an additional hazard. 'His
technique,' wrote one reviewer, 'is not quite what it was, which
is hardly surprising in a man of his age'. Although Alkan's
command was still equal to the toughest sonatas of Beethoven
and Chopin and could encompass the intricacies of Bach's
organ fugues played on the *pédalier*, he may, at sixty, no longer
have felt himself physically capable of the terrifying and
sustained demands of his own most powerful works.
Significantly enough, he had no hesitation in including such

large-scale chamber compositions as the Violin and 'Cello Sonatas with their taxing piano parts. Could it be that the presence of a distinguished colleague like Franchomme gave the composer Dutch courage during these later years?

Bertha claims that the series of 'Petits Concerts' came to an end in 1877 with the premature death of Gustave, but recent research suggests that Gustave died five years later. It now seems that the concerts may have been phased out over a season or two.* Almost certainly however, the last complete series was that of 1877 and, as if to make amends for the deprivation of the preceding year, a special concert was organised in Alkan's honour on January 21st. The programme included his *Duo for Violin and Piano* and the *Second Concerto da Camera*, accompanied by a distinguished quintet of strings. Before launching his final season of 'Six Petits Concerts' Alkan was also persuaded to give a preview in the Salle Pleyel on February 14 to which the public and press were admitted. 'Nothing could be more interesting' wrote the *Revue et Gazette* 'than this glimpse of the history of the piano as summarised by M. Alkan's playing. The most characteristic pieces from all centuries and of all the masters from Couperin and Scarlatti to Schumann are reviewed and each is played in the style appropriate to it and with the expression which suits it. In M. Alkan we still find those supreme qualities we have so often had occasion to praise', and a week later: 'The gallant artist is now gathering encouraging proof of public esteem and interest in his work'.

At last Alkan was receiving, in some small measure, the recognition that had somehow, always eluded him: but, inevitably, at sixty-four and in poor health, the colossal effort of preparing and giving this yearly series could not continue indefinitely. The last concert of the 1877 season may not have been his final bow to the Paris public but he was soon to return to the shadows of an even greater obscurity than before.

---

*Dennis Hennig, in an Oxford B.Ph. thesis completed in 1975, claims that a certain number of 'Petits Concerts' did indeed straggle into the 1880's, after a further break in 1879. He adds the interesting information that Alkan even included a performance of the complete *Solo Symphony* on 18 April, 1880. This was not, however the work's première. A certain Mademoiselle Poitevin, a former pupil of Delaborde, had already introduced both *Ouverture* and *Symphonie* to Paris audiences in 1876 and '77.

10 The Final Years

Unlike Alkan's earlier periods of reclusion our scanty knowledge of his final years suggests that even the urge to compose must now have dried up. Despite their high opus number *Les Mois* op. 74 and the *Trois Grandes Etudes* op. 76 are reprints of early works, and the virile little *Toccatina* is also probably not as late as its Opus number of 75 suggests. Most likely Alkan's last compositions were the 4th and 5th *Recueil de Chants* op. 67 and 70 which were almost certainly completed by the time the 'Petits Concerts' were launched in 1873.

During his brief return to the limelight it had occasionally been possible to coax Alkan to appear as guest of honour at a social gathering, a brave but risky undertaking for the organisers. Inscrutable and unpredictable he was quite capable of taking his leave before the party got into full swing; even while distinguished guests, anxious to meet the celebrated artist, were still arriving. According to Bertha, Alkan was a most lively conversationalist, expressing himself with delightful ease on an inexhaustable variety of topics. Unfortunate were those caught up in the full flight of an absorbing discussion with him as the clock struck ten for then, surely enough, Alkan would make his exit brusquely and without apology, leaving the group in bewildered embarrassment. He was, of course, almost grotesquely fastidious about time-keeping; witness the precision with which each item is timed in programmes advertised to begin a 'Neuf heures très precise'. Even so, ten o'clock does seem to have held a special, even mystical fascination for him; one has only to remember the bell-like strokes which introduce the 'prayer' towards the end of the third movement from his *Grande Sonate*.

Alkan, doubtless, paid a high price for his social indifference. He was an artist who instinctively recoiled from the obligation of getting to know the 'right' people and the one time he had repudiated his natural inclinations by seeking their help the effort had foundered and humiliated him. Bertha tells us that as late as 1879 Alkan still harboured a deep and bitter grudge against Marmontel 'for whom he had been sacrificed at the Conservatoire'. As a result, he was convinced he had been robbed of the chance of being decorated — the supreme honour normally reserved only for those who occupied an official position. Bertha decided to draw attention to this injustice and approached a highly influential diplomat, Prince Orloff, husband of one of Alkan's favourite pupils, who promised to set matters right at once. With one leap the enthusiastic Bertha was at the Salle Erard to inform Alkan: but he felt surprised that beneath an outward show of gratitude the older musician looked both displeased and humiliated. The Prince went to Alkan's house nine times without finding him 'at home'. For his part Alkan felt obliged to return the visits also nine times but failed to meet the Prince. Finally he was told by the usher that it was useless to come in the afternoons as His Excellency always left at 2.00 p.m. 'How tiresome' replied Alkan 'I like to rest after my meal' ... and the Légion d'Honneur fell by the wayside. Bertha seems to have been strangely insensitive: Alkan should never have been told about such an initiative. How, one wonders, might Beethoven have reacted in similar circumstances?

Unabashed, the doughty Bertha again allowed himself to become involved in an attempt to satisfy another of Alkan's unfulfilled desires. Towards the end of his life the old man became ever more convinced that there was a plot afoot to defraud him of his life's savings. Suddenly he made up his mind that he would give everything to the Conservatoire for the foundation of a chair in the instruction of the *pédalier*. Once made, the decision was final and irrevocable. On Alkan's behalf, Bertha approached the administration and a meeting was arranged. On the appointed afternoon Bertha and a high official of the Beaux Arts waited, but in vain. The meeting broke up in embarrassment and a few minutes later Bertha discovered his old friend at Erard's calmly seated at his piano.

His excuse was simple. He had changed his mind.

The difficulty of approaching Alkan in these last years is graphically underlined by the experience of Friederick Niecks, for twenty-three years Reid Professor of Music at Edinburgh and the author of a classic biography of Chopin. When, in the summer of 1880 Niecks visited Paris, the sixty-seven year old composer was one of the musicians whose acquaintance he was most anxious to make. What happened is so strange and so enlightening that it must be told in full and in Niecks's own words:

'Having heard much of his strange ways and the difficulty of approaching him, I procured a letter of introduction from a friend of mine who, during a sojourn of several years in Paris, had wooed the shy artist with unusual success. But even thus armed I knew that I was undertaking an enterprise that called for much circumspection. After careful consideration of the possibilities of a safe plan of campaign, I decided to begin by calling at his house. My question whether M. Alkan was at home was answered by the concierge with a decisive 'No'. To my further enquiry when he could be found at home, the reply was an equally decisive 'Never'. And in spite of all the expenditure of diplomacy and eloquence I lavished on the powerful functionary, this was all the knowledge I could obtain. My next move was to write a respectful and propitiatory letter to the great man, asking for an interview, and enclosing our common friend's letter of introduction. The result of this petition materialized into a missive such as was perhaps never before received by mortal man. A brief scrawl of a note, written on an odd scrap of paper, stuck into a cheap envelope. The handwriting so shaky that it could be described only by the epithet vermicular, and the style so curt and awkward that it was impossible to say with certainty whether the writer was rude or clumsy in expression. But the predominant effect of the letter on the receiver was that of a hard repulse. The next time I saw Mme. Dubois, she asked me how I had fared with Alkan. I told her my doleful tale; but instead of condoling with me, she laughed and thought my story good fun. 'What are you going to do next?' she asked. 'Do next?' I asked, much surprised. 'How can I, after having been so rudely repulsed, take another step to approach him? I must respect his desire, and preserve my self respect' 'No, no; nothing of the kind. He plays every Monday and Thursday at Erard's. You go there, without ceremony, and make him a fine speech — don't talk of Chopin, talk of Alkan'. The advice went much against the grain, but Mme. Dubois' powers of persuasion overcame my reluctance. The next Monday or Thursday found me soon after three at Erard's. The spacious room, apparently used for solo recitals and chamber music, had no other furniture than chairs and two instruments — an ordinary grand piano and a pedal grand. There were present Alkan playing, and two listeners, a lady and gentleman — English, I think. As soon as the master had finished the piece in hand he rose to meet me. I felt somewhat nervous. How would he receive me? But my fear was soon dissipated. His reception of me was not merely polite, but most friendly. And what was my astonishment when after a few formal words the venerable white-haired, white-bearded, stooping (almost hunchbacked) old man began to talk freely and with the greatest amiability about Chopin and other matters. In fact, it came out that the reason of his reluctance to see me was hyper-conscientiousness — he was afraid that the information he could give me was not important and accurate enough'.

Although still in his sixties one has the impression of a very old man: yet the rigorous routine of Alkan's life continued, unchanged, for a further eight years. Day by day, immaculate in black frock coat, white cravat and top hat he would arrive at the Salle Erard where his room was always reserved. Week by week he would fetch his produce from his favourite shop in the Halles-Centrales district of Paris: nothing would entice him to entrust such sacred matters to a paid servant who, he would argue, must inevitably swindle him. As ever, he continued to prepare his own meals using only ingredients of the highest quality, and despite his solitary life would always eat at a neatly-laid table placed next to his piano. The composer's great-nephew, the artist Jacques Nam who died in 1974 aged ninety-three, was taken as a boy to visit the great man. He vividly remembered his uncle as 'un vieux célibataire' who bowled paper balls under his pianos and his bed in order to check that the cleaner was not scrimping her work. Madame Rachel Guerret, Jacques Nam's sister, and herself a fine miniaturist is, happily, alive and well at ninety-seven. She actually remembers being taken by her grandmother, Céleste Marix (née Morhange) to hear her great uncle play at the Salle Erard, presumably at one of his Monday or Thursday matinées. As she was seven or eight at the time this must have been during his last years and although she was too young to comment on the performance she clearly remembers that Alkan habitually played in the old-fashioned position with his back to the audience.

Those who survive a life of sickness often find the resilience to face old age with equanimity. Alkan might well have continued to play his *pédalier* well into the next decade had it not been for the bizarre, and possibly apocryphal, event which, until recently, had seemed so essential a part of the whole Alkan legend. His death, on 29th March 1888, is so entangled with contradiction that it requires a chapter on its own.

11 The Death of Alkan

No event in Alkan's singular life has been savoured with greater
relish than the one which is generally believed to have ended it.
'He was found crushed beneath his upturned bookcase from
which he had been extricating a Hebrew religious book' ... and,
as if to confirm the solemn nature of Alkan's final act we are
told that he was discovered still clutching the *Talmud*, his
beloved book of Jewish law, which is traditionally kept on the
top shelf so that no other book can be sacrilegiously placed
higher. Fate could hardly have contrived a more apt conclusion
to a remarkable life and so entrenched is the story of the falling
bookcase that the drab suggestion that Alkan might, after all,
have died like other men, of heart failure for instance, comes as
nothing short of an affront. For this reason alone, those few
scholars who had chanced upon Alexandre de Bertha's article
about the composer, published in 1909, had conspired to keep
silent on his disconcertingly mundane account of Alkan's death:
that is until Hugh Macdonald spilt the beans in a persuasive
challenge to the whole bookcase theory in the *Musical Times* of
January 1972. This is Bertha's description of Alkan's end as
quoted by Mr. Macdonald, 'He was found stretched out, lifeless
in his kitchen in front of his stove which he was probably about
to light to cook his evening meal having spent the afternoon as
usual at Erard's'. At first glance his version could hardly be
more sober and concise but it neither tells us how Alkan died nor
who discovered him, and Bertha's preceding sentence, not
quoted by Mr. Macdonald., suggests that the possibility of an
accident cannot be ruled out even in the context of this account:
'He died suddenly on the 30th March 1888 in a situation caused

by his unusual habits'. Bertha may, of course, simply mean that there was no one at hand to help the old man when he collapsed, but the ambiguity of this account and an error about the date which was, of course March 29, does make one wonder if Bertha actually had first-hand knowledge of the event.

The earliest published suggestion that Alkan did not die naturally appeared in H.H. Bellamann's article of 1924, in which he baldly states: 'An accident in his apartment caused his death'. This and later variants of the same story are all traceable to the same source, Isidore Philipp, who gave a full account of Alkan's death to Robert Collet in 1937. Philipp, who at twenty-three had already embarked on the teaching career which was to make him famous, claimed to have been one of the party that dragged Alkan's body from beneath the bookcase. As Philipp was also responsible for other unique snippets of information about Alkan, such as his relationship with Delaborde, it is important to examine his reliability. Phyllis Sellick studied with him and knew him well. That he could be capable of such a deception, even in jest, was to her out of the question. Robert Collet renewed his acquaintance with him shortly before Philipp died in 1958, aged ninety-four. Collet does not consider it in Philipp's character to concoct such a story but admits that he was a marvellous raconteur with a penchant for grotesque detail. He obviously relished the bookcase story which he related clearly and specifically. The seemingly naive embroidery that Alkan was reaching for a Hebrew religious book need in no way discredit Philipp's account. As we have seen, such books are customarily lodged in high places and Alkan was constantly referring to them. He was also short and bowed. Philipp, seeing the toppled bookcase would immediately put two and two together. The macabre claim that Alkan was still clutching the Talmud is surely a colourful later addition and not to be taken seriously.

Surviving members of the Alkan-Morhange family also confirm Philipp's account. Both the grand-children of the composer's sister, Céleste, who were nine and seven when Alkan died, remembered their great-uncle well. Neither had ever questioned the cause of his death and Madame Guerret who, at ninety-seven, is the last surviving link with the composer, has sent the author several valuable souvenirs. She is quite definite about the nature of his death: 'Oui à ma connaissance c'est bien son armoir qui lui est tombé dessus et qui a causé sa mort'. So dramatic an end to her celebrated uncle's life would undoubtedly have captured the imagination of a young child and remained firmly engraved on her memory.

Unfortunately, quite apart from Bertha's article, there still remains one serious obstacle to our acceptance of the famous legend. The police archives contain no record of an accident, and so it seems that the whole mystery is still wide open. Is it conceivable that a violent accidental death could be hushed up? ... and if so, why? On the other hand it seems just as unlikely that Philipp would have passed on so absurd a story unless he had good cause to believe it himself. Hugh Macdonald's canny suggestion that the ever resourceful Delaborde sold Philipp the tallest of tall stores about his father is a non-starter. Not only was Delaborde out of Paris at the time of Alkan's death but he did not show up at the funeral either, and this brings us full circle to the final paradox in this whole enigma. Apart from the immediate family only four mourners were present at Montmartre Cemetery that bleak, wet Easter Sunday afternoon of 1st April 1888. These were the coffin-bearers consisting of Blondel, head of Erard's, the violinist Maurin ... and the authors themselves of these two contradictory accounts of Alkan's death: Bertha and Philipp.

12 Rescue of a Lost Cause

As Alkan was being buried with full Jewish rites, the Paris musical world was expressing surprise that he had lived so long. 'He had to die' wrote his obituarist 'in order to prove his existence'. This cynical epitaph to Gallic indifference becomes the more ironic when one remembers that, despite his solitary habits, it had been possible those last fifteen years to slip quietly into Erard's any Monday or Thursday afternoon and eavesdrop on one of the greatest masters of the keyboard of his century. Yet, apart from his own strictly confined circle, Alkan had remained an outsider. His creative genius had largely passed unrecognised. Even his fitful efforts to promote himself as a pianist were either too little or too late to make any real impact. Alkan had become a lost cause: an artist who had 'locked away a talent' which might have brought honour to his country. The French do not easily forgive those who fail to acquit their debt to society. Now they banished Alkan to the archives as one of those 'interesting historic figures' whose identities melt so conveniently into the shadows of their immortal contemporaries; and there he would undoubtedly have remained had it not been for the powerful advocacy of two men.

The first rescue-operation was mounted at the turn of the century with a series of Alkan performances by Busoni in Berlin and with the re-printing by Costallat in Paris of many of his important piano works. The inspiration behind this massive project came from Isidore Philipp who chose the music, wrote a stimulating preface and persuaded the reluctant Delaborde to add his illustrious name as co-editor. For once Alkan was in luck. His music was re-printed from the original plates and its startling appearance, so different from that of any other composer, is a constant reminder both of its originality, and of the pains he took over the clarity of its presentation. Copyright problems alone explain the regrettable omission from Costallat's generous catalogue of the *25 Preludes* op. 31, the *Etudes Majeurs* op. 35 and the *Grande Sonate*. Happily all these works have recently become available and M. Gérard Billaudot, who has taken over the Costallat edition, has ambitious plans for a complete Alkan edition in the foreseeable future.

Meanwhile, in the German capital, Busoni was infuriating the reactionary critics by including such works as Alkan's implacable study *En Rythme Molossique* from op. 39 and several of the Etudes Majeurs at his historic recitals in 1901/2 and 3. 'Preposterous French rubbish' was how they dismissed the satirical Military Caprices, op. 50 and the *Allegro Barbaro*, a virile octave study on the white notes alone. These Berlin critics, already hostile to Busoni for his championship of Liszt, looked upon this latest discovery ... and French at that ... as the last straw. Busoni returned to the attack in 1906 by playing Alkan's cadenza in a performance of Beethoven's *C minor Concerto*. How, one wonders, did they contain themselves as this monstrous *tour de force* reached its peroration converting the Concerto's opening theme into a famous tune from the Finale of the Fifth Symphony? The mind boggles. As a peace-offering Busoni handed them Alkan's Grande Etude for the Left Hand Alone from op.76, but the olive branch was not taken. It is tempting to believe that Busoni set about baiting his critics with sardonic glee, but artists are irrationally sensitive to adverse notices and when, twenty years later, Philipp challenged him to give further Alkan performances he remembered the Berlin critics and refused. Busoni, it seems, had played the wrong music in the wrong place at the wrong time.

Despite hostility in Germany and apathy in France the mere fact that an artist of Busoni's authority was playing Alkan began to arouse interest in the music and curiosity about the man. Several articles spread over the next thirty or so years attempted, with varying success, to assess the one and satisfy the other. We have already referred to Alexandre de Bertha's reminiscences of 1909 and to Niecks's description of his meeting with Alkan published in the *Monthly Musical Record* of January 1918. Both Bertha and Niecks also included a brief discussion of the music, the former showing little understanding of Alkan's creative originality and regarding his true value as that of a custodian of tradition. Niecks, on the other hand, made a close study of the works published by Costallat, quoting the opinions of Schumann and Liszt on the early compositions. He seems reluctant to commit himself, however, and argues that where there is neglect on the one hand there must surely be shortcomings on the other. 'Perhaps', he suggests 'Alkan's talent was speculatively inventive rather than spontaneously creative.'

A fuller discussion of the music was published in the American *Musical Quarterly* during 1924. The writer, H.H. Bellamann discovered much that excited him. *Morte* op. 15, for instance, with its 'great bell effects and rolls of muffled drums', and the *Etudes Mineurs*, op. 39, which he found 'completely astounding'. Unfortunately Bellamann, like Niecks before him, could never have heard these works performed by a real virtuoso. No piano music is more misleading in appearance than Alkan's especially as he approaches the climaxes of such movements as *Quasi Faust* from the *Grande Sonate* or the finales from his Sonatine, Concerto and Symphonie for Solo Piano. These baffling pages 'black with marching regiments of notes' become in performance a Pandora's Box of demonic power to which only the most fearless player holds the key. Bellamann's opinion that the *Grande Sonate* would never be performed, his curt dismissal of the marvellous *Trois Petites Fantaisies*, op. 41 and his comparison of the great Study for Left Hand Alone from op. 76 with a transcription by Sydney Smith, suggest that, like many others, he was deceived by the very look of the notes on paper. Is it not significant that the only musicians of the period who accepted Alkan as a great composer were themselves great performers: Busoni, for instance, who had no hesitation in placing him alongside Liszt, Chopin, Schumann and Brahms as one of the five greatest post-Beethoven writers for the piano. Now came an uncompromising affirmation of this greatness in a remarkable book by a remarkable man.

Kaikhosru Sorabji is reputed to be a complete virtuoso. Certainly, if he can play his own astonishing piano music, perhaps the most difficult to have been published this century, he must be. No student of Alkan is now unfamiliar with the arresting opening of Sorabji's compelling essay on the composer's works as it appeared in his book *Around Music* in 1932: 'Few remarkable and astounding figures in music have been the subject of such persistent misunderstanding, denigration and belittlement as Alkan'. Of the Etudes, op. 35 and 39 he has this to say: 'These amazing works place him among the great masters of piano music ... the prodigious, teeming richness of invention the vivid originality, the very individual harmony, the superb mastery of these works cannot be too highly admired'.

Three years later Bernard van Dieren in *Down Among the Dead Men* was making equally spectacular claims, but whereas Sorabji had praised the epic, the uncanny, the grotesque and the sardonic, van Dieren was more concerned with the descriptive and psychological elements in Alkan's music. Commenting on *Le Tambour Bat aux Champs* (The drum beats a salute), one of the two *Capricii* op. 50, he writes: 'I seriously doubt whether there is another short composition which, in an equally simple form, conveys so overwhelmingly a sense of concentrated tragedy'. Such powerful advocacy as that of Sorabji and van Dieren could not pass unheeded and in 1938/9 the B.B.C. invited Egon Petri to give three Alkan recitals in commemoration of the fiftieth anniversary of the composer's death and the 125th of his birth. Petri, like his teacher Busoni, had all the intellect, temperament, size and technique to match this demanding music. In these historic broadcasts he included two of Alkan's largest solo works, The Symphonie and Concerto from the *Etudes Mineurs* op. 39. It is interesting to note that Petri's pioneering performance of the Solo Concerto took fifty minutes which suggests that on this occasion, at least, he cut several of the seventy-two pages of its gigantic first movement. The London critics were sharply divided about the quality of this unfamiliar music: one was ecstatic, while another considered it 'a monumental fraud'. Petri's recitals are still vividly remembered as a landmark in pre-war music broadcasts and he would undoubtably have recorded some of Alkan's major works had it not been for the intervention, in 1939, of the Second World War. Even fifty

years after his death, it seems, Alkan could still fall victim to his
inherent bad luck. Within a few months of Petri's last broadcast
the composer's fate was once more vested in the hands of a few
cognoscenti, mainly pupils of Petri and Philipp both of whom
were now living in America. There, interest would doubtless
have grown more rapidly but for the serious illness, in the early
'forties, of Petri himself.

* * * * * *

Artistic climates rarely survive a cataclysmic social upheaval.
Post-war Britain sought musical consolation in the comparatively cool detachment of the Baroque revival and a fugitive quest
for pure style in the classics. Inevitably, the bold romantic
gestures and massive sonorities of the nineteenth century rang
hollow in a world still dazed by its own epic struggle. For the
next two decades Alkan became one of the casualties of a hostile
musical environment. His own single-handed crusade to bring
baroque and classical masterpieces before a pleasure-seeking
Paris public in the 1870's was, of course, quite unknown: in fact,
the very little that was still known about Alkan now associated
him with the very byways and backwaters of nineteenth-century
virtuosity he had himself so resolutely opposed. Is it surprising
that in so alien an atmosphere his torch flickered, reluctant;
that his admirers, forced on to the defensive, sounded muted
and apologetic in their anxiety not to overstate a doubtful case?
Performances became few and far between and one brave
attempt to re-kindle interest, a B.B.C. series in the late 1940's,
took place in the early experimental days of Third Programme
before it could reach a wide audience. Yet even in this, Alkan's
darkest hour, his admirers waiting patiently in the wings for the
passing of a generation, there came a revolution in the
gramophone industry which was to grant him an ally perhaps
more formidable than the verbal or pianistic persuasions of a
Sorabji or a Petri.

   In 1960, a young and enterprising gramophone company
invited the author to record the first long-playing records of
Alkan's music including both the Symphonie and Concerto for
Solo Piano. As it turned out the courageous policy of this
enlightened company was premature and before the project

had taken wing *Triumph Superfi* was in the hands of the Receiver. Meanwhile Alkan had found a passionate, fiery and committed evangelist on the other side of the Atlantic: a man with a mission and the sense of occasion to promote it.

Raymond Lewenthal had studied with the colourful Olga Samaroff, an erstwhile pupil of Delaborde at the Paris Conservatoire, and so Lewenthal could claim the distinction of being a great grand-pupil of the composer himself. He now set about giving recitals and broadcasts of Alkan's music, providing a highly entertaining commentary to an excellent new edition of his works, writing a long-promised book about the composer, but, most important, recording several of his masterpieces including the Symphonie for Solo Piano. At last a young and unprejudiced audience could judge for themselves this legendary piano music which had so long remained seen but not heard. This new generation was already acclaiming the Symphonies of Bruckner and Mahler: pianists were discovering through the re-issue of historic gramophone records, the undreamt-of technical powers of some of their nineteenth century precessors. Played for all it is worth Alkan's Solo Symphonie can be a shattering pianistic experience. It also anticipates in a most startling way the music of Brahms, Bruckner and Mahler. Reaction to Lewenthal's performance was immediate and decisive. 'Some of the writing is prophetic' wrote Harold Schonberg in the *New York Times*, 'some is inspired: all of it attests to a remarkable imagination'.

Britain was quick to respond to the American initiative and an L.P. devoted to a quite different aspect of Alkan's many sided talent, his genius as a miniaturist, appeared in 1969. 'He has a mind of astonishing originality' wrote Roger Fiske in *The Gramophone*: but this selection of short pieces was only a preliminary canter. In January, 1970, one hundred and thirteen years after its publication, came the first recording of the gigantic Concerto for Solo Piano and any lingering doubt about Busoni's claim that here was one of the five greatest composers for the piano since Beethoven was silenced. Leading critics greeted the work as 'a masterpiece ... intriguing, eccentric and disturbing;' as 'the most difficult piano work of its century and one of the most original'. In a perceptive article in *The Times,* (14th March, 1970) Stanley Sadie draws particular attention to 'the curious mixture of extreme severity and profound passion that characterises this music'. 'What of the actual style?' he continues. 'It is not easy to describe, still less easy to compare with others. The *tutti* sections are tough, severe, dramatic music utterly unlike anyone else's ... possibly the most remarkable passage comes in the first movement's development section, with cold, granitic textures, austere harmonies, the music poised and motionless. The Concerto has an Adagio starting quite conventionally, but constantly devolving on to the keyboard's extremes, with the left hand suggesting funereal drum beats and there is a Finale of demonic energy, music of extraordinary dark power and fiendish difficulty.'

The unique technical demands and the sheer size of such compositions as the *Concerto*, the *Grande Sonate* and the *Trois Grandes Etudes* op. 76 must inevitably forbid their frequent public performance. By the mid-1970's, however, a sizeable proportion of Alkan's major works for piano has become steadily available on record. When the first complete recording of the *Grande Sonate* was released in 1974 it was at once acclaimed as a masterpiece indispensable to an understanding of nineteenth century piano music as a whole; yet this work had taken a hundred-and-twenty-five years to reach the public. Can it be that Alkan's message, stark and uncompromising as it is, has more relevance today than it had for his own generation a century ago? Is this the strange case of an artist using the language and techniques of one period to communicate with another? Significantly enough his music appeals to musicians of widely contrasted persuasions. It has recently been rumoured that Dr. Gordon Jacob is working on an orchestral paraphrase of the brilliant *Festin d'Esope* Variations from op. 39 and, apart from such long-standing admirers as Busoni, Sorabji and Humphrey Searle, a growing number of contemporary British composers, including Robert Simpson, Alan Ridout, Ronald Stevenson, John McCabe and Roger Smalley are all discovering something unique and vital in Alkan's many-sided genius.

* * * * * *

If recognition of Alkan's genius in Britian and America was
delayed by nearly a century, so far as his native France was
concerned he might just as well never have existed. During this
same period of eighty or so years — an era which witnessed the
successive triumphs of Fauré, Debussy, Ravel, *Les Six*, Messiaen
and Boulez — Alkan's eclipse was total and enduring. Unlike his
younger contemporary, César Franck, whose creative career
made similarly little impact during his lifetime, Alkan left no
distinguished pupils, such as Vincent d'Indy, to rally round his
cause after his death. Despite his vast repertory, Delaborde no
longer peformed his father's music and we do not even know if
Alkan continued to teach during those last, shadowy, years.
Probably it was no longer necessary for, despite his earlier
complaints of trying to scrape a meagre living from teaching, he
left a sizeable estate of 100,664 francs. Some of this money was
left to Jewish charities such as the Conservatoire Israélite. 'Elie
Miriam dit Delaborde' received a small annuity of 400 francs;
but by far the most interesting bequest was the following: 'to the
music section of the Institute': (ie. the Conservatoire)
1) Annual sum of 800 francs for the foundation of a yearly
   competition for *pédalier*.
2) Annual sum of 1,800 francs for the foundation of a yearly
   competition for the composition of a cantata (conditions to
   be expressed by the executor of his Will).

Even now, though, Alkan's desire to make his posthumous
peace with the institution that had rejected him was frustrated.
The secretary of the Conservatoire informed his lawyer that the
Institute could not accept the two legacies.

At Alkan's bequest, furniture and presumably other chattels
passed to his sister Céleste and the surviving brothers
Maxime and Napoléon, who was also entrusted with his
music.*

But for a brief mention in Bertha's reminiscences, Napoléon,
the most celebrated of all Alkan's next-of-kin, would seem the
most obvious custodian of his brothers' unpublished works.

---

*Isidore Philipp told Robert Collet that he managed to acquire Alkan's
pédalier but that his neighbours complained so bitterly that he was
forced to part with it. No wonder Alkan had found it expedient to
maintain two flats, one above the other.

Bertha informs us, however, that the two musicians were
permanenly 'at daggers drawn', and for reasons neither was
willing to divulge. It is certainly odd that Napoléon, fine pianist
that he was, took no part in the 'petits Concerts'. As we have
seen, Alkan had enjoyed his brothers' collaboration back in the
1840's, and Napoléon had, for his part, championed Valentin's
earlier compositions. Perhaps Alkan was vexed that this
younger brother, whom he had taught and encouraged, had
succeeded just when he had failed; for Napoléon had become
the most academically distinguished of the entire, gifted family.
His long, illustrious reign as head of the Solfège department at
the Conservatoire was crowned in 1895 by the Légion
d'Honneur. 'How furious Alkan would have been' wrote Bertha
'had he lived to witness the decoration of his younger brother
Napoléon'. Alkan's legacy to Napoléon of 1,000 francs,
however, must mean that the brothers had eventually buried
their differences, and this is also borne out by the handing-down
in Napoléon's family of such personal souvenirs as Alkan's *Prix
de Rome* medallion and the beautiful early portrait by Dubufe.

Jean-Yves Bras, is convinced that Alkan's manuscripts were,
indeed, entrusted to Napoléon and that any search for the
missing *B minor Symphony* should start on this assumption. In
1906, the eighty-year-old Napoléon, wealthy owner of three fine
Paris houses, married his housekeeper, Eva Flesch, but died a
few months later. Eva was a staunch Catholic, and this alone
must have proved a stubborn obstacle to their earlier marriage.
It seems probably that one of Napoléon's final acts was to grant
full legal status to their two children, Adolphe and
Emma-Christina, aged thirty-three and twenty-seven, as well as
to the woman who had been his wife in all but name. On
Napoléon's death his music library, including his brother's
manuscripts are believed to have passed to his son, Adolphe, a
brilliant concert-pianist but, strange to relate, Adolphe only
survived his father by a few months. He also died in 1906, quite
suddenly, quite unexpectedly of septicaemia, after being
thrown from his horse. That his wife was having an affair at the
time and that she married her lover not long after the event adds
a speculative dimension to the whole tragedy. Family
recollections of an auction sale at which Adolphe's personal
effects were disposed of suggest that Alkan's manuscripts may

have been dispersed. During the German invasion of France, in 1940, other valuable papers in Emma-Christina's possession were hastily stuffed into a tin chest and buried in the garden of her country home. After being occupied by German officers the house was eventually sold. No attempt has yet been made to recover the box and so its possibly valuable contents remain for the moment tantalisingly out of reach.

In the early 1970's, prompted, no doubt, by Alkan's rising star in Britain and America, French radio (the O.R.T.F.) mounted an important series of discussions and performances of his music in the course of which a plea was broadcast for information about the possible whereabouts of manuscripts, including the missing Symphony. The sole response was from the artist, Jacques Nam, who came forward as Alkan's great-nephew. Although unable to produce the elusive manuscripts he represented a further branch of Alkan's family, that of the composer's sister, Céleste, the artist's grandmother. Through Céleste's two daughters, Marie and Albertine, the musical and artistic traditions of this remarkable family have been passed on to the third and fourth generations. Marie sang at one of her uncle's 'Petits Concerts' in the 1870's and her husband, a Morhange cousin, kept a flourishing musical instrument shop in Paris at which a prize exhibit was a harmonium invented by Céleste's husband, Mayer Marix. Both Albertine's children became distinguished artists. Madame Rachel Guerret, now in her late nineties, was a fine miniaturist while Jacques Nam's remarkable portrayal of cats, familiar to collectors of Sèvres porcelain, won him the Légion d'Honneur, as well as the admiration of Colette.

Like his cousin, Delaborde, who was as celebrated a painter as he was a musician, Nam had a flair for animals, including monkeys (remember Delaborde's pet apes!). Jean-Yves Bras, who was fortunate enough to have met Jacques Nam during his last years was enchanted by his personality, fascinated by his reminiscences of the Alkan family and captivated by his long memory of artistic life in the capital. It is to the author's great regret that he missed him. Just as a meeting had been arranged by the O.R.T.F. in Paris, illness struck. He died soon afterwards, aged ninety-three, having lived to see the music of the great-uncle he had always remembered so vividly at last catching the imagination of their fellow countrymen.

13   Personality and Appearance

Eye-witness accounts of meetings with Alkan, confined as they are to his later years, all agree that there was something quite unusual about his personality. 'He had a most impressive presence', wrote Niecks who had met the composer in 1880, 'the face of a noble Jewish type, the capacious head and the penetrating and refined expression all spoke of the thinker. And the venerable appearance of his presence was heightened by his dress which was clerical in cut and colour.' Marmontel drew a similar picture. 'His glance was shrewd, a little sly ... his stooping gait and puritanic dress give him the appearance of an Anglican minister or Rabbi'.

Alkan spent his entire life in the more secluded parts of Paris clinging tenaciously to the sober dress and stiff formality of the July Monarchy of Louis-Philippe (1830-1848), the age of his youth. In many ways he sensed himself an intruder into the second half of the nineteenth-century and must have felt utterly lost amidst the gaudy extravagances of the Second Empire. Perhaps it is not entirely by coincidence that the reign of Napoleon III (1852-1870) also marked the boundary of Alkan's largest and most decisive withdrawal from what he considered an increasingly tasteless, meretricious and alien society; a society in which artistic ambition seemed to be ever widening its horizons by lowering its sights. He became more and more puzzled and disillusioned. Commenting on Gounod's success in Germany he asked Hiller if his fellow-countrymen had fallen into their second-childhood. Of Hiller's own latest productions, however, now utterly forgotten, he exclaimed 'It warms my heart to know some good work is appearing in the face of so

much muck. I mean it, so much muck. How can there be so
many to make it and so many to take pleasure in it?' This was in
1859, a year before Alkan dragged himself, in his own words: 'as
a matter of duty for a misanthropic musician ...' to Wagner's
concert on January 24 1860. 'It was worth it' he declared 'for my
indignation. What brutality, what base materialism'.* His
delight, on the other hand, in the compositions of such
contemporaries as Mendelssohn and Schumann shows that 'sour
grapes' was not at the root of his hostility towards Wagner. Such
is the measure of Alkan's objectivity that although he utterly
rejected the music of his friend Liszt, who had earlier supported
and encouraged him, he sprang angrily to the defence of his
own harshest critic when 'some high-priest of criticism too
imbecile to understand or appraise him' classified Schumann
with the new school of 'Wagner, le Listz [*sic*] and Co.'

Of Alkan's basic modesty there can be no doubt. One may
scan the wide-ranging Hiller correspondence in vain for all but
a glancing reference to his own work. Not one word, for
instance, about the historic publication of his monumental
Studies op. 39, in 1857. Yet Alkan is constantly asking for
details about his friend's compositions, and his letters are
liberally peppered with astute asides about other people's
music. As we have seen, his programmes tended to leave room
only for a modest group of his own shorter pieces amidst an
array of those great, unfashionable classics in which he so
ardently believed, but which he knew would bring him neither
fame nor fortune. Alkan's accusation of 'base materialism' in
Wagner's music is a significant indication of his own puritanic
attitude to life in general and to music in particular. Four years
later, after attending the first performance of Rossini's
swan-song, The *Petite Messe Solennelle*, he described it as 'the
work of a genius, but a genius called Rossini: from the religious
point of view, Vulgo — Anti-Christ'.

---

*Many other musicians, including Auber, whom Wagner admired, found
his music both derivative and vulgar. Their own artistic framework,
which stemmed from Cherubini, was far too severely circumscribed to
allow them to enter such an erotic and highly-charged emotional
world. In any case, an orchestral concert consisting of 'bleeding chunks'
could only have seemed to dot its dreadful i's and cross its terrible t's,
while giving little indication of Wagner's true stature.

The little we know of Alkan's religious outlook — his
scepticism over Liszt's admission to Holy orders, his habit of
translating the New Testament and his spontaneous use of the
expression 'Anti-Christ' — all these point to the free-thinker
unlikely to pay lip-service to established creeds, whose deepest
convictions express themselves in private study rather than
through public gesture. 'How is it we have never discussed
religion together?' he asked Hiller, a professed agnostic, in
1866. 'I don't mean Christianity or Mosaism, but *Religion*.' On
the other hand Alkan's profound knowledge of the Old
Testament together with his constant study of the Talmud
made him an authority on Jewish law. 'He has the learning as
well as the appearance of a Rabbi', wrote Marmontel, who also

Alkan in his last years
(Oil painting by Rubach; courtesy The Musical Times*)*

emphasised Alkan's solitary, insatiable thirst for knowledge. His all-embracing culture must have stemmed from shrewd observation and wide reading and even thirty years after Chopin's death he was still expressing concern over his friend's lack of intellectual curiosity. 'Chopin was not a reading man' he told Niecks in a deprecatory tone. 'Pierre Leroux, the philosopher and socialist who loved him tenderly, brought him all the books he published, but his friend left them unread, nay, uncut. Victor Hugo's writing he did not like, nor George Sand's.'

'The reputation Alkan had as an intellectual we already saw documented in his face' wrote Niecks; and this is confirmed by all three of the best known portraits of the composer. The most familiar is a medallion reproduced on the outer cover of the Costallat edition of his music; the most impressive, an oil-painting by Wilhelm Rubach, of Alkan's eagle-like profile, looking for all the world like one of the ancient Hebrew prophets. But with the pencil sketch shown on page 91, we enter once more the inescapable realm of mystery and paradox that colours so many aspects of his affairs. The National Library of Canada, who acquired this portrait as part of the Percy Scholes collection, claims that it is signed and dated on the back: 'A. Osborne Campbell, 1926'. But this makes nonsense, unless the artist, about whom nothing seems to be known, copied it from an earlier source. Yet there has never been the slightest evidence for the existence of a full-face portrait from Alkan's later years, and his quaint reticence before the camera makes the possibility of a lost photograph singularly unlikely.

'We will not confine ourselves to a description of Alkan's appearance as he is depicted in certain photos,' wrote Marmontel in 1877, 'that is, taken from behind'. As though to lend substance to Marmontel's strange assertion just such a long-lost photograph has recently come to light. It is reproduced on the front cover. Why should Alkan refuse to expose his 'intelligent and striking physiognomy' to the camera? Was he inordinately shy? There happens to be one, slender, piece of evidence from his teaching days at the Conservatoire that he might have been. In a dissertation undertaken at Harvard University in 1941, its author, J. Bloch, relates how Alkan used to peer furtively out from his studio, drawing back,

Medallion of Alkan
(Bibliothèque Nationale, *Ottawa, Canada*)

hastily, should he catch sight of someone in the corridor. Only when he was quite sure the offender had disappeared would he make his own exit. Unfortunately Bloch gives no reference for this curious example of Alkan's unsociability. If the story is true, it may have been handed down by either Philipp or Petri, both of whom were in America at the time Bloch was writing.* But, to shed a clearer light on Alkan's reticence before the camera we must turn once more to the Hiller correspondence. Commenting on a recent photograph he had just received from his friend, Alkan explained why he could not reciprocate. 'La postérité' he declared 'se passera donc de mes traits sacrés et de mes sacrés traits' — this was in 1863, when he was approaching fifty. Although his sly play on words defies translation, the meaning is clear. Posterity, would have to do without knowing what Alkan looked like ... and the explanation? ... His last two or three appointments with a photographer had coincided with such misfortunes that he dared not tempt Providence again.

As it happens, Alkan did not completely cheat posterity of his photographic likeness. The full-face, but undated portrait

---

*As early as 1844, Joseph d'Ortigue, a close neighbour of Alkan in the Square d'Orleans, had described him as shy but craggy; diffident and too proud to seek public favours.

Pencil sketch of Alkan by A. Osborne Campbell
(Bibliothèque Nationale, *Ottawa, Canada*)

(page 92) shows him relaxed and seated on a chair handed down in Napoléon's family, and adorned with a gigantic button-hole. Like the back-view photograph it was discovered among Jacques Nam's family souvenirs and has now been presented to the Bibliothèque Nationale in Paris. So firmly entrenched is our traditional image of the world-weary old recluse, as he is depicted by Campbell, that this comparatively youthful presentation of him may come as a surprise. If so, it will certainly require a further degree of mental adjustment to turn to the little known pastel portrait by his friend Edouard Dubufe (1820-1883) showing Alkan as he must have looked around the time of those early concerts with Chopin and Liszt. Like his brother-in-law, the composer Gounod, Dubufe had married

Photograph of Alkan
(Courtesy of Bibliothèque Nationale, *Paris)*

Pastel portrait of Alkan by Dubufe
(Courtesy of Madame Dora Ray and Madame Jacqueline Cuzelin)

one of Zimmerman's four daughters and it is a mark of the
famous teacher's esteem for his favourite pupil that he asked
Dubufe to capture the young virtuoso's striking features just as
he was embarking upon a brilliant public career — albeit a
career that was soon to wither and die that he might fulfil his
greater, if less glorious destiny.

14   The Reluctant Virtuoso

Alkan's reputation as one of the greatest pianists of the nineteenth century is remarkable, for apart from the evidence of his fantastic piano writing it rests, solely, on the testimony of his colleagues. With the vague exception of his two youthful visits to England, which passed unnoticed, he was never heard outside Paris, and even then. only in strictly limited circles. Within these narrow confines Alkan's concert career falls naturally into three periods; the young virtuoso who retired at twenty-five, four sporadic appearances as pianist-composer during his thirties, and his phoenix-like return to the concert platform in 1873.

Until his long retirement in 1849 Alkan's technique was probably second to none and it is, doubtless, the young virtuoso whom Liszt remembered when he told Frits Hartvigson, himself a well-known pianist, that Alkan possessed the finest technique he had ever known but preferred the life of a recluse. Marmontel, in his *Histoire du Piano* (1885), gave a further twist to Liszt's remark: 'Owing to his horror of fuss and publicity' he wrote 'Alkan has lived misanthropically; but all those musicians capable of appreciating him consider him a genius!' The slight note of reservation hidden in the phrase 'those musicians capable of appreciating him' may supply one of our clues to Alkan's lack of public acclaim. As the supreme guardian of the French *style sévère* his playing was noted for its clarity, sobriety, logic and Gallic tightness of rhythm. A gramophone record made in 1904 by the sixty-nine-year-old Saint-Saëns playing excerpts from his pocket concerto, *Africa* gives a very good idea of the virtues and limitations of the *style sévère* as it survived into the twentieth century. The high speed clarity is remarkable, the rhythmic drive stimulating, the control undeniable: yet the criticisms of Alkan's own early playing, that it was cold, that it lacked 'breadth, poetry, passion and imagination' could just as easily be directed against the veteran Saint-Saëns, on the evidence of this recording alone: and remember, Saint Saëns was one of those artists Alkan invited to play with him at his 'Petits Concerts'. The attributes of transparent honesty, detachment and total lack of self-indulgence so often admired as the hallmark of maturity are just as frequently frowned upon in a younger artist as his 'lack of emotional involvement' or his inability to 'see beyond the notes'. The young Busoni was dubbed 'an intellectual without a soul', and the not-so-young Schnabel dismissed, in some quarters, as a 'scholarly' pianist. Although certain critics of Alkan's earlier playing may have been similarly blinded by its ruthless intellectual glare, no one, one hastens to add, denied him his absolute mastery.

The most casual glance at the scores of such works as the *Etudes Mineurs* suggests that double-notes, octaves and the most towering conglomerations of fat chords were to Alkan what scales and arpeggios are to lesser mortals. His colossal technique, however, was never paraded and, consequently, only his fellow pianists could have had any idea of the feats being accomplished before their eyes and ears. One has, altogether, the impression of a lofty, somewhat puritanical artist: the bringer of light rather than warmth or, as Léon Kreutzer intimated, the musicians' pianist rather than the public's idol.

Besides his uncompromising integrity, the austerity of his programmes and the general lack of glamour associated with his concerts, there may have been a further aspect of Alkan's public performances that could sometimes have reduced his power to woo the Paris audiences. Léon Kreutzer spoke of his occasional loss of 'inspirational freedom' when playing in public, blaming it on the pianist's fierce campaign against the affected, the exaggerated, etc. But perhaps Kreutzer's diagnosis is wrong. Maybe the root cause of Alkan's lack of spontaneous inspiration on the podium should be sought elsewhere, within his highly complex, hyper-sensitive, vulnerable psychological make-up —

that dangerous compound of authority and humility, conviction and doubt, fervent enthusiasm and basic caution which must on occasions have robbed him of the armoury so vital to those who appear in public. Despite his fabulous facility and wonderful memory, one has the impression that he was never really at home on the concert platform. It is not always appreciated that anxiety in the prodigiously well-equipped performer is seldom apparent in loss of technique but tends to manifest itself in other ways: over-speeding and lack of equilibrium in some cases, decrease in warmth and an exaggeration of the cerebral aspect in others. This may well have happened with Alkan throughout his life. Furthermore, as his fastidious timings suggest, he was probably the 'definitive' rather than 'inspirational' type of artist, his interpretations representing a crusade towards an ideal conception rather than an impromptu, never-to-be-repeated gesture. Although no great performance is possible without both discipline and inspiration, in Alkan's case, if he were not 'on form', the inspiration would probably have evaporated leaving only the discipline.

At his best, Alkan must have been a unique pianist combining all the finest attributes of the French school — its equality of touch, clarity, lucidity and rhythmic severity with the intellectual penetration of a Busoni. Little wonder even Liszt, himself, is reputed to have felt ill-at-ease when playing in his presence! Reviewing the 1849 concert which preceded his long absence from public life, the seventy-year-old Henri Blanchard tried to describe Alkan's style — its energy, fullness, clarity, refinement and sensitivity. He spoke of graduations of sound which Alkan possessed to a remarkable degree and considered his ability to stir the emotions by applying the singer's art to the keyboard as 'a modern conquest'. Marmontel was similarly impressed by Alkan's infinite variation of touch which, together with his uncanny sense of style, enabled him to re-create the music of widely differing periods and schools, giving to each work — be it Scarlatti, Couperin, Mozart, Beethoven or his contemporaries Schumann, Mendelssohn and Chopin — its own distinctive character. Again, Marmontel stressed Alkan's rigorous and rhythmic precision which scorned the abuse of *tempo rubato*, that lingering freedom of pulse, so closely identified with Chopin's playing, which had become almost universal by the second half of the century.

It is doubtful, however, if any musician was more familiar with Chopin's playing or more qualified to comment on it than Alkan himself, and his factual account of it can hardly be ignored. 'Not only did Alkan answer all my countless questions about Chopin's playing' wrote Bertha 'but he played me all his immortal friend's masterpieces one after another, and more than once. He initiated me into most of the secrets of Chopin's playing which were lowered into the grave with him sixty years ago' — Bertha was, of course, writing in 1909 — 'They compel one to the conclusion that Chopin should never be treated as a romantic or a revolutionary but, on the contrary, as a staunch classicist who had, involuntarily, opened up new frontiers of his art which had lain dormant until his arrival. Consequently a classical style of playing is imperative to the correct interpretation of Chopin's music. The decorations, however inspired, must not be treated as accessories but rather as part of the whole fabric of the composition. It also follows that the *tempo rubato* the majority of pianists impose wholesale upon Chopin's music is only valid where expressly indicated by the composer. To underline the truth of this assertion Alkan would repeat again and again Chopin's own axiom that 'the left hand must act as conductor, regulating and tempering any involuntary inflexions of the right hand.'

Alkan considered Chopin's nuances inimitable, for, owing to his lack of physical strength, he obtained his gradations by an infinite extension of his *piano*. Alkan concluded that although an ample sonority has its rightful place in Chopin's compositions, the exaggerated *fortissimo* with which certain modern virtuosi assail the ear is utterly out of place in his music and can only destroy its homogeneity'.

So far as Alkan's own playing of Chopin was concerned Bertha admired its comprehensive technical command but felt it was slightly lacking in brilliance and elegance. It may be that a profound study of the German classics had gradually weaned Alkan from the graceful polish and facile glitter of the Paris salon style to a more monumental breed of pianism appropriate to the sober polyphony of Bach or the rugged austerity of late Beethoven, the twin gods of his later years. Or was it, simply, that his fearsome technical armoury and icy precision that must once have chilled the heart of many a famous rival was, after a quarter of a century of comparative neglect, already on the wane by the time Bertha knew his playing in the 1870's — the period of the 'Petitis Concerts'? Once or twice during the reviews of these concerts we may detect small reservations which suggest that his technique no longer supplied him with a complete insurance against the stresses and strains of nervous tension and the additional burden of ill-health.

'It was obvious' wrote *La Revue et Gazette* 'that indisposition was robbing the artist of his ability at his third 'Petit Concert'. This was in 1873 during his first season. Alkan's bowed and aged appearance in his sixties indicates the encroaching hazard of rheumatism which would, doubtless, have affected his hands. Even so, in Marmontel's opinion his 'magisterial command' at sixty-four was unimpaired. How, one might ask, did Marmontel know this in 1877? Had he run the gauntlet by slipping into one of the 'Petits Concerts' under the eagle-eyed surveillance of Gustave Alkan? Fortunately there are other reliable accounts of Alkan's playing during those later years which substantiate Marmontel's claim. The pianist was already in his late sixties when Niecks heard him on the occasion of his second visit to Erards. 'About a dozen ladies and myself formed the audience' wrote Niecks 'and we had the privilege and pleasure of hearing him play for nearly two hours compositions of his own, of Mendelssohn, of Bach, and of Bach-Vivaldi. Much of this music he performed on the pedal-piano, of which he was very fond and for which he wrote a good deal (for instance op. 64, 66, 69, and 72). Of the character of his truly masterly playing I remember this. It was free from any kind of extravagance and of over-accentuation of his individuality: loyalty of interpretation seemed to be his chief aim. Firmness, repose, and sobriety in rhythm and dynamics struck me as outstanding features. But the playing was as much distinguished by the clearness of phrasing and the richness of delicate shading, as by the avoidance of the abuse of *tempo rubato*. The legato element may be said to have been the predominant element. In the main I agree with Marmontel's estimate of Alkan's admirable style of playing, inclusive of some austerity, "the austerity that suited his Puritan and convinced nature".'

'In the intervals and at the conclusion I had some more delightful conversation with Alkan — during which his face was now and then illumined by a kindly, sly smile — of which I remember especially our discussion of Bach's arrangement of Vivaldi's *Concertos*, in which, and its relation to the originals, he was greatly interested'.

Niecks's emphasis of the *legato* element in Alkan's playing at this time is rather interesting. Many of his earlier works, and some from his maturity, seem to demand a highly pungent and detached style of playing — The *Allegro Barbaro* and *Le Festin d'Esope* spring immediately to mind. One wonders, again, if his pre-occupation with Bach's organ works, played on the *pédalier*, had led Alkan to change his earlier style in favour of a smoother manner of performance.

The most authoritative musician who heard Alkan towards the very end of his life was Isidore Philipp, himself a brilliant virtuoso familiar with the playing of all the greatest pianists of the era, from Liszt to Busoni. His impression of his uniqueness as a performer never faded. In response to the spontaneous requests of his listeners, claimed Philipp, Alkan, now in his seventies, would still find no problem in drawing from the vast store-house of his amazing memory works of every period from Couperin to Chopin. Philipp gave Robert Collet the impression that, in these familiar surroundings, at any rate, Alkan's technique had remained equal to anything.

But what, exactly, were the surroundings in which Philipp, and perhaps Madame Guerret as a small child, remembered hearing Alkan? The more one ponders on the vague and sometimes conflicting accounts of his last appearances at Erards the greater becomes the impression that, apart from his private bi-weekly matinées, some kind of fitful concert activity continued, possibly in the form of invitation-recitals, to the end of his life. Philipp spoke of 'elegant gatherings' frequented by 'des dames très parfumées et froufroutantes'. Who were these elegant, perfumed ladies with their rustling skirts? Were they all that remained of Alkan's highly selective audience 'the audience of great artists?' The following extract from the early recollections of Vincent d'Indy contains the veiled suggestion that the 'Petits Concerts', themselves, may have continued in some form or other, right up to the time of Alkan's death. But, quite apart from speculation about his possible concert activities during these later years, the whole account is of unusual interest. Not only does it throw a unique light on Alkan's playing and personality in the mid-1870's as it impressed this highly sensitive and informed musician, but it is also psychologically revealing, coming as it does from an avowed anti-semite writing just fifty-five years after the event:-

'One day I was passing by the small rooms on the first floor of the Maison Erard, reserved only for great pianists, for their practice and lessons. At the time the rooms were all empty, except one, from which could be heard the great *Triple-Prelude* in E flat by Bach played remarkably well on a *pédalier*. I listened, riveted to the spot by the expressive, crystal-clear playing of a little old man, frail in appearance, who, without seeming to suspect my presence, continued the piece right to the end. Then, turning to me: 'Do you know this music?' he asked. I replied that, as an organ pupil in Franck's class at the Conservatoire, I could scarcely ignore such a fine work. 'Play me something' he added, giving up the piano stool for me. Although somewhat over-awed, I managed to play quite cleanly the *C Major Fugue* — the one affectionately known as *The Mastersingers* because of its similarity to a certain Wagnerian theme.

Without comment he returned to the piano saying 'I am Charles-Valentin Alkan and I'm just preparing for my annual series of six 'Petits Concerts' at which I play only the finest things'. Then, without giving me a moment to reply: 'Listen well, I'm going to play you, for you alone, Beethoven's *Opus 110* — listen ...' What happened to the great Beethovenian poem beneath the skinny, hooked fingers of the little old man I couldn't begin to describe — above all in the Arioso and the Fugue, where the melody, penetrating the mystery of Death itself, climbs up to a blaze of light, affected me with an excess of enthusiasm such as I have never experienced since. This was not Liszt — perhaps less perfect, technically — but it had greater intimacy and was more humanly moving ...

'Without giving me a chance to speak, Alkan shoved me violently over to the window and looking straight into my eyes, pronounced these words — words which are precious to me and whose well-meaning bluntness I have never forgotten: 'You —

you're going to be an artist, a real one ... farewell, we will not see each other again ...' Indignant, I protested that I would be in the front row at his next 'Petit Concert'. He replied, more sadly: 'No, we will never see each other again'.

Some compulsory occupation connected with my life in Paris prevented me from being present at the first 'Petit Concert'; on the evening of the second I had an engagement in the provinces; other obstacles on the third. In short, several years passed before I managed to find a free evening and then, at the moment I was about to go to one of these concerts, I read in a paper that Charles-Valentin Alkan had just died'.

15   The Music

A companion volume will be devoted to an examination and analysis of Alkan's music but the present work would seem sadly incomplete without some discussion of its style and flavour.

It would be surprising if the amazing wealth of contradictions that colour Alkan's character did not enrich his creative work. Indeed, the very diversity and range of his compositions has proved a frustrating obstacle to the filing-cabinet mind. Like Beethoven, he seldom if ever repeats himself. His music belongs to no recognisable school, period or place; and it stubbornly refuses to wear its convenient label of identity. To start with, Alkan's harmonic language itself presents a paradox. On the surface he is a severe conservative whose purpose is well served by the harmonic small change of such contemporaries as Mendelssohn and Schumann.

To the unprepared ear he can sometimes sound impersonal — even faceless; his lyricism charming, but faded. On the other hand, his disturbing and unpredictable use of this familiar language may seem freakish, foreshadowing the wilful eccentricity of certain twentieth century composers like Satie and Ives. Apart from Alkan's genius for parody and caricature, such an impression is wholly misleading. Imagine the entire output of Berlioz being withheld until the late twentieth century and then appearing in the impersonal black and white dress of the solo piano. Would he not emerge as a similarly perplexing and controversial figure — and for the same reason, that his language is conservative, his manner radical? Alkan has, in fact, been dubbed The Berlioz of the Piano but although kinship of spirit and background is sometimes obvious, to label him thus is deceptive. Alkan did not care for Berlioz's music. He can be understood only on his own terms and resemblances to the many other composers, earlier, contemporary or even later with whom he has been compared are useful only as descriptive guidelines. Ultimately they melt away.

Alkan's music is romantic, in the Berlioz tradition — highly imaginative, colourful, pungent, displaying a sober, unsensuous but deeply moving lyricism — yet within a framework firmly rooted in the classics. His large-scale structures reveal a profound, almost instinctive awareness of the subtlest inflections of sonata-form as understood by Haydn, Mozart, Beethoven and Schubert. A constant and supple variation of phrase length adds tensile strength to his paragraphs — a characteristic he may well have inherited from Haydn. He establishes his mood immediately: witness the desolate drum beats at the outset of his *Funeral March* op. 26 (1844) or the laconic opening of his splendid *Minuetto alla Tedesca*, a work which seems to combine characteristics of Bach, Haydn, Mozart and Beethoven in a crucible of originality. This piece also displays a bold, uncompromising style of piano writing typical of him. We know, from accounts of his own playing, that Alkan would take the most fearsome hurdles in unflagging tempo. Certainly anyone listening to the relentless finales of his *Solo Concerto, Symphonie* or *Sonatine* for the first time must experience an exhilarating sensation of something unique in piano writing, for here virtuosity is the outcome of a white-hot creative energy. In the finales of both the *Symphonie* and *Sonatine* the musical argument could hardly be more cogent. Not a note is wasted and they both have an obsessive, almost suicidal drive.

If Alkan's language is basically diatonic, simple and direct — even severe — his manner can be startling. Take, for instance, the *Allegretto in A minor*, one of his *Chants* from op. 38. It looks just like Mendelssohn: but the whole piece is obsessed by an inner pedal point. The sub-mediant note F, repeated 414 times, cuts icily into its texture producing some powerful clashes. In the final bar it hovers, suspended, having established a tenuous stability of its own. Several of the *Chants* (there are five sets of six pieces published between 1857 and 1877) give the impression of Mendelssohn gently refracted in the distorting mirror of Alkan's mind. The *G minor Barcarolle*, for example, contains some quaint inflections which give a plaintive ambiguity to the tonality, as though Gershwin had re-written one of Mendelssohn's *Songs without words*.

Against an almost naively simple background Alkan will sometimes plunge into an alien, comfortless environment — a region of disquieting darkness. This happens with uncanny effect in the *Scherzo-Minuetto* from his *Sonatine*, op. 61, where one is led by a series of baffling modulations into a bleak twilit world of suspended tonality. Still more astonishing is the middle section of the fourth in his *Onze Pièces dans le Style Religieux* op. 72, where, without warning, a brief page full of the darkest fantasy occurs. The left hand gropes in widely spaced intervals like a 'cellist in search of a tune, while a monotonous ostinato rises and falls above an obstinately recurring pedal note. The effect is both eerie and hypnotic, and quite unlike anything else of the period — or of any period, for that matter. Doubtless it was passages such as these that Sorabji had in mind when he wrote in *Around Music* (1932) of that 'eerie, bizarre and somewhat eldritch quality that makes this master's work so irresistable'. Sorabji also emphasises satire as an essential ingredient of Alkan's style, describing the brilliant military parody *Capriccio alla Soldatesca* op. 50, as a 'piece of grotesque mocking caricature'. A less abrasive species of grotesquery spills over into the little-known and delightfully freakish *Funeral March for a Dead Parrot* scored for mixed voices, three oboes and bassoon, which dates from the same year, 1859. At the anguished climax of this masterly study in mock pathos, the voices become afflicted by a continucus, wailing lament. Yet a casual glance at the score reveals the strictest fugal discipline beneath the grief-stricken counten-ance, for Alkan's structural sense is never more vigilant than when he is givng fullest rein to his emotions. The satirical vein in Alkan can be studied in essence in a singularly bizarre miniature entitled *Les Diablotins*, one of his *48 Esquisses* op. 63. A constant pattern of parallel tone-clusters foreshadowing the experiments of Henry Cowell is twice interrupted by an unctuous hymn-like fragment marked, according to its register, *quasi santo* and *quasi santa*. So strange is its appearance in print that Alkan has been accused of writing 'paper music'.

Of all his miniatures the *Esquisses* are probably the most consistently rewarding. There is hardly one of these little pieces which does not explore some curiosity of texture, harmony or rhythm, and several — the *First Love Letter*, for instance — suggest a shrewd and quizzical awareness of the subtlest of human relationships strangely at odds with our traditional image of the man. The series ends with an impressive *Laus Deo*, one of a large number of specifically religious pieces which appeared throughout his life and culminated in the splendid *Prières* op. 64 for *pédalier*. Several of these display an overtly Hebraic element, a further essential ingredient of the composer's complex style and one which will be explored in the companion volume. The jubilant optimism of some of these pieces is an added reminder of how little we still know about Alkan's real character.

If his smaller pieces display a bewildering variety of moods and styles, the sheer range of Alkan's output as a whole must prove still more disconcerting to those who would seek to pigeon-hole him. How are they to reconcile the quaint charm of a three-line fragment like *Les Cloches* (also from op. 63) with such epic structures as the great piano studies op. 39? These gigantic works, disarmingly entitled *Douze Etudes dans Tous les Tons Mineurs*, appeared in 1857. Although published six years after the final version of Liszt's Transcendental Studies, they are as far removed from these as Liszt's are from Chopin's. They are, in fact, studies in the production of orchestral textures and sonorities on the piano. Three of them constitute the three movements of the colossal *Solo Concerto* recently described by Roger Fiske as one of the most original piano works of its century. Four more comprise the *Symphonie for solo piano*. As each study is in a progressively darker minor key (C, F, B flat and E flat), the whole work gives a prophetic impression of the 'progressive tonality' of Mahler and Nielsen. Each movement also becomes progressively shorter: the first, sombre, impassioned and powerful, has already been admired for its striking anticipation of Brahms; the second is an impressive funeral march; the third a rough-hewn minuet with a haunting trio; while the Finale has been aptly described by Raymond Lewenthal as 'a ride in hell'. The final study from op. 39, *Le Festin d'Esope*, is a fantastic and colourful set of variations 'stuffed with every conceivable device of keyboard fiendishness', in the words of Peter Stadlen.

The tremendous scope of Alkan's op. 39 studies has tended to overshadow the op. 35 set in all the major keys and published ten years earlier. This is a pity. While in no way on the same epic scale they contain, nevertheless, some remarkable pieces. The seventh — a descriptive fantasy entitled *Fire in a Neighbouring Village* — has been compared to Berlioz, but it also invokes some of the childlike power of Beethoven's *Pastoral Symphony*. The fifty study — the furious *Allegro Barbaro* — may have given Bartok the idea for his own piece of that title. Despite the key signature of F major this virile octave study is entirely on the white notes, its outlines crudely sharpened by the harsh B naturals.

Like the *Etudes Majeurs*, Alkan's *Grande Sonate* op. 33 also dates from his early thirties. That it could remain, for well over a century, little more than a tantalising legend is a sad and disquieting commentary on professional indifference. In many ways it is the most significant piano sonata of its age. Certainly, as Raymond Lewenthal has rightly claimed, it is the strangest one until the Ives sonatas. Doubtless, many virtuosi glancing through its forbidding pages would blench at the daunting prospect of ending so epic a work with two slow movements. But, as William Mann has pointed out, this strange layout in no way spoils the formal balance or hangs a millstone round its musical effectiveness. The four movements of the sonata are headed *twenty*, *thirty*, *forty* and *fifty* years and each corresponds to that particular stage in a man's development. The first, a whirlwind scherzo, seems to represent the ebullient man of action seeking maturity. The second, subtitled *Quasi Faust*, unleashes a pianistic eruption of unprecedented fury. The black, satanic forces that sweep through this gigantic movement are controlled, contained, and finally exorcised by a central chant-like motif which forms the basis of a fugal exposition of bewildering complexity. Hushed, mysterious, it seems to float outside time itself. In a riot of sharps, double sharps and a unique treble sharp, it modulates to the arctic region of E sharp major in a spider's web of eight independent parts plus three doublings — eleven sharps and eleven voices in all. The peroration which follows is vibrant with the peal of celestial bells as the movement approaches its triumphant conclusion. If domestic bliss, portrayed in Alkan's third movement *Un Heureux Ménage* provides the perfect foil to *Quasi Faust*, the finale is its malignant sequel. Sub-titled *Prométhée Enchâiné* it is prefaced by seven lines from Aeschylus's *Prometheus Bound*. Here principal ideas from earlier movements are reduced to their essence in a rondo of uncompromising severity, powerful as granite; implacable as fate.

As we have seen, a first encounter with Alkan's music can produce a variety of reactions. The very stuff it is made of — its relentless drive, its cutting dissonances, the tart astringency and brusqueness of such pieces as the *Minuetto alla Tedesca*, the finale from the *Sonatine* or the *Allegro Barbaro* — will find little response among those who would seek a cosier breed of Romanticism. Again, the stark gulf that separates the mocking satire of *Les Diablotins*, for example, from the brooding loneliness of *Prométhée Enchâiné* can come as a disturbing shock to those as yet unprepared for such widely contrasting styles.

First impressions are similarly divided about the design or uniqueness of Alkan's major works, though few would deny them their vast range and power. For instance, the opening bars of the solo *Concerto* compel attention, but until one has become familiar with the movement as a whole an uneasy impression may well persist that the driver has lost his way or is taking an unnecessarily circuitous route. A stranger to Bruckner can be similarly deceived by his far-flung strategy and unaccustomed expansiveness — the very qualities in fact, which, until recently, proved so severe a stumbling-block to appreciation of Schubert's spacious forms. On the other hand, some of Alkan's finest works have a Beethovenian terseness; the *Sonatine* and the *Solo Symphonie* are succinct examples. In these cases, however, owing to a classical objectivity, their originality may only reveal itself on repeated hearings. Busoni and the Danish symphonist Carl Nielsen sometimes present a similar problem. At first, the substance can seem unworthy of the conception; an impression which tends to dissolve on deeper acquaintance. The casual listener, or the impatient one, may find himself deflected towards other aspects of the composer's bewildering diversity —

the quaintly pictorial or the satirical elements for instance —
and decide that, after all, Alkan is simply the odd-man-out of
his times; a fascinating eccentric — slightly mad, perhaps,
whose grotesquery merely provides a smoke-screen for his
inherent anonymity.

It is part of Alkan's fascination, of course, that he can
command such widely conflicting opinions. It must not be
forgotten, however, that although the mists which have so long
enveloped his genius are at last being dispelled, the picture that
emerges is far from complete. Much of his piano music,
including the *Trois Grandes Etudes* op. 76 and most of the
Etudes Majeurs op. 35, beckon us impatiently. Among the *25
Preludes*, the *30 Chants* and the *48 Esquisses* there is a goldmine
of miniatures waiting to be plundered. Some of these lie well
within the grasp of the fluent amateur and many of the *Preludes*
and *Esquisses* would provide the younger pianist with a
rewarding introduction to his larger works.

The compositions for *pédalier*, alas, present their own unique
problem; but how is it possible that Alkan's splendid chamber
music continues to remain silent — above all the wonderful
Sonate de Concert op. 47, for 'cello and piano? A performance
by two great artists should prove a revelation for it is possibly
Alkan's most personal and impassioned work. Cast in four
broadly conceived movements it opens with a luminous Allegro
full of bold, soaring outlines but shot through with darker
turbulence. The second movement is an enchanting *siciliano*
and the third a meditation on the following quotation from the
Old Testament prophet *Micah* (Ch. 5, verse 7); ' ... as a dew
from the Lord, as a shower upon the grass, that tarrieth not for
man, nor waiteth for the sons of men ...' Words cannot convey
the rapt, mystical atmosphere of this central adagio in which a
haunting 'cello soliloquy invokes passages of strange, unearthly
beauty as the piano floats and shimmers above hypnotically
repeated pizzicati. By contrast, the finale is a devilish,
pulverising *saltarello*, calculated to raise any audience to its
feet. It is a matter of urgent concern that works like the *'Cello
Sonata*, the *Duo for Violin and Piano* and the powerful *Trio*
should be publicly performed and recorded. One word of
warning, though: like all great music Alkan's demands
masterly and dedicated playing. Anything less would be

sacrilegious and damaging to his cause.

Demand for his music is growing. Informed critical opinion is open-minded and favourable. In short, the stage is set. If the enigma of his lonely life can never be completely explained, there now seems every sign that the veil of mystery that has so long engulfed so much of Alkan's music will soon be completely and finally lifted.

Bibliography

Bellamann, H.H.
  The Piano Works of C-V Alkan (Musical Quarterly, 1924)
Berlioz, H.
  Memoirs (Tr. & Ed. by D. Cairns: Gollancz, 1969)
Bertha, A. de
  Ch.-Valentin Alkan aîné; Etude Psycho-Musicale (Bulletin Francais de la Société Internationale de Musique, 15 February 1909, pp 135-47)
Busoni, F.
  Foreword to the *Collected Edition of Liszt, vol.1*
Chopin, F.
  Selected Correspondence (Tr. A. Hedley: Heinemann, 1962)
Davis, Lawrence
  César Franck and his Circle (Barrie & Jenkins, 1970)
Dean, Winton
  Bizet: His Life and Work (Dent, 1965)
Delacroix, E.
  Journal (Ed. A. Joubin, 1932)
Dieren, B. van
  Down Among the Dead Men (1935)
Fétis, F.J.
  Biographie Universelle des Musiciens (1st Edition 1837-1844; 2nd Edition 1860-1865)
Hallé, C.
  Autobiography (Ed. M. Kennedy, 1972)
Harding, James
  Gounod (Allen & Unwin, 1973)

d'Indy, V.
> *Impressions Musicales d'Enfance et de Jeunesse: III Adolescence* (Les Annales Politiques et Litteraires, 15 May 1930)

Lewenthal, R.
> *The Piano Music of Alkan* (Schirmer, New York, 1964)

Liszt, F.
> *C-V Alkan: Trois Morceaux dans le Genre Pathétique op. 15* (Revue et Gazette Musicale, October 1837)

Macdonald, H.
> *The Death of Alkan* (The Musical Times; Jan 1973)

Marmontel, M.A.
> *Les Pianistes Célèbres* (1877)

Murdoch, W.
> *Chopin: His Life* (1934)

Niecks, F.
> *Personal Recollections. Ch.V. Alkan* (Monthly Musical Record, Jan. 1918, pp. 4-7)

Piggott, P.
> *The Life & Music of John Field* (Faber & Faber, 1973)

Schonberg, H.G.
> *The Great Pianists* (Gollancz, 1964)

Schumann, R.
> *Music and Musicians: Essays and Criticisms* (Tr., Ed. and annotated by F.R. Ritter; 2nd Series, 1880)

Searle, H.
> *A Plea for Alkan* (Music & Letters; 1937, pp 276-279)

Sitwell, S.
> *Liszt* (Appendix I: A Note on Alkan; Faber & Faber, 1937)

Sorabji, K.S.
> *Around Music* (The Unicorn Press, 1932)

Index

Index of Alkan's works mentioned in this volume

List of Illustrations

FAMILY-TREE OF ALKAN MORHANGE

(Confined to those mentioned in this volume)

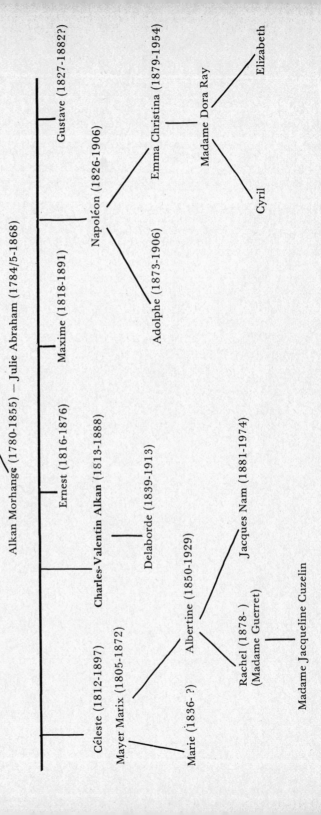